[GOING WIDE]

Self-Publishing Your Books
Outside The Amazon Ecosystem

An Author Your Ambition Book

M.K. Williams

ISBN: 978-1-7333929-7-6 (Paperback)
ISBN: 978-1-952084-10-2 (eBook)

Library of Congress Control Number: 2021914500

Printed by M.K. Williams Publishing, LLC in the United States of America.

Interior Formatting by Formatted Books

First printing edition 2021.

authoryourambition@gmail.com
www.authoryourambition.com

Works by M.K. Williams

Fiction
The Project Collusion Series
Nailbiters
Architects

The Feminina Series
The Infinite-Infinite
The Alpha-Nina

Other Fiction
The Games You Cannot Win
Escaping Avila Chase
Enemies of Peace

Non-Fiction
Self-Publishing for the First-Time Author
Book Marketing for the First-Time Author
How to Write Your First Novel: A Guide
for Aspiring Fiction Authors
Going Wide: Self-Publishing Your Books
Outside The Amazon Ecosystem
The Fiology Workbook

Dedication:

*To all the aspiring authors who dream, plan, write,
and work hard to make their books a reality.*

CONTENTS

PART 1

The Wide World of Books

Without fail, every time I talk with a new author, I get the same question:

"How can I get my book on Amazon?"

For authors who want their books to get in front of millions of users, this is a very smart question.

Since 1994 Amazon has been training all of us to associate their brand with books. I remember when I was a child, sporting my dorky glasses and a mascara lightning bolt on my forehead, and anxiously waiting for the midnight release of the next book in my favorite series. The late-night parties at our local bookstore were tons of fun! But my mom wasn't about to wait in line until 1 am to buy the book. No, she had already done her homework.

Bright and early the next morning (I had crashed into bed the moment we got home), I woke up to a wonderful brown cardboard box that had my copy of the book. I dove right in and read as long as I could, determined to find out what happened next. Who magically delivered this must-have book to my doorstep the day the book was released? None other than Amazon.

Yes, in a world where books once had to be purchased in a brick-and-mortar store with limited space in their stock room, Amazon made it possible to get any book you wanted. Then they added Prime and you could get it the next day. Then they released the Kindle and you could get it right now!

Amazon became synonymous with books. While their business has grown to include much larger, and more profitable lines of business, those of us who write and publish books have one retailer at the top of our list: Amazon.

With each author I have helped over the years, they always ask about getting their book onto the Amazon website first. A great starting point, but only one part of my philosophy as an author and publishing coach. I always have my book available as many places as I could handle, making sure to reach my audience wherever they are, and I help others do the same.

As I started to help more and more authors, I noticed a new trend. I began to get questions about how they could expand to get their books on the shelves of other stores, both physical stores and other online marketplaces. Many authors go all in on one strategy, only to find that wasn't the best one for them. They felt short-changed because they had missed an opportunity. They were frustrated at the hoops they would have to jump through in order to select a different path now and expand their reach outside the Amazon ecosystem.

I can't blame them. There are endless articles online teaching people how to publish on Kindle, make thousands on KDP, or hack the Amazon algorithm. Some experts are dedicated to only instructing their following on how to self-publish with Amazon. But what about other avenues? When so much of the information available to new authors focuses on just one platform, it can be difficult to learn how to get a book into other retailers. For those of us looking to write as a career, we know we have to get our books to the readers wherever they are. And not all of them are on Amazon.

As I grew older and had to fund my book addiction with my own money, I soon realized that my library card might as well be one of those coveted American Express Black cards that all the coolest celebrities had back in the early 2000s. With a library card I could read any book I wanted, whenever I wanted. The power went to my head. And when it was time for me to self-publish, I knew I had to have my book in the library system. Amazon couldn't get me there, and they can't get you there either. This was the origin of my journey as a "wide" author. (I'll talk about this later in the book.) I had to find this information one step and one question at a time. I had to go wide before that was a term indie authors were using.

Publishing with multiple platforms to get your book out to the most readers, has been around as long as Amazon-exclusivity has been around. It has been the counterpoint and alternative for years. As an indie author, I noticed that the rhetoric around publishing across a broad spectrum of platforms really ramped up in 2019 and more authors wanted to go wide than ever in 2020. I found this to be a wonderful shift in thinking and appreciated having more clients asking me about this option. But several came to me after they decided to go wide by uploading their book any-where and everywhere. They signed up with every direct platform and every aggregator. *All of them. **All. Of. Them***. Headaches and frustration ensued. I could only do so much at that point to help correct some of the problems created, most of the solutions had to work through the customer service department at each individual platform. Yikes.

I tell you this because I want you to avoid these headaches. I want you to be able to self-publish your book for maximum reach and impact without undue stress or anxiety. I want to help you go wide without stretching yourself too thin.

For authors who have already listed their books exclusively with Amazon, this book will guide you on how to get your book out to more retailers. For writers who have their first completed manuscript ready to self-publish and are looking for a game plan to publish-wide, this book will help you learn which Amazon-exclusive programs to avoid.

In this book we will go over the benefits of this strategy, the platforms that you can leverage, the technical steps that you need to take, and most importantly, how to sell more books using this strategy. Let's dive in so we can start laying the foundation for your big expansion outside of the Amazon ecosystem.

CHAPTER 1

Why Go Wide?

You may have already answered this question for yourself, hence you picked up this book. Or you may have heard about this concept after a month of low sales on Amazon and decided to make a switch. That frustration can be great fuel to find a better solution, but it is weak fuel. It won't carry you through the hours of work that going-wide requires. That is why first, we are going to really dial in on why you want to make this change. Is it just about the additional opportunities to earn royalties, or is there some other motivation? Not only will defining this ambition help you stay on track, but it will be critical to selecting the right mix for your books.

So, let's get to the first question:

What does "wide" even mean?

In general, publishing wide is defined by its counterpart, Amazon-only. There are many strategies for self-publishing and optimizing the Amazon platform that focus on listing your book exclusively with Amazon. You're committed, you're not seeing other people. Wide means you aren't exclusive and are seeing other people, you're self-publishing on platforms outside the Amazon ecosystem.

When I refer to the Amazon ecosystem, I am referencing Amazon Kindle Direct Publishing (KDP) and Audiobook Creation Exchange (ACX) which gets your book onto Amazon.com (and associated country sites like .ca, .co.uk, etc.) and Audible.com.

Ask a dozen different authors their wide publishing mix and you'll get a dozen different answers. There is no one strategy that I can prescribe in this book that will work for every author who picks it up. It just isn't possible. For starters, some genres do better in different mediums than others. Then we need to consider what level of work you as the author are willing to do and what you have to invest in your author business. (Not just in terms of money, but effort as well.) Do you have an ambition to translate your book into multiple languages? Do you have the stamina to pursue a brick-and-mortar strategy? Sure, we all want those things. We all want to be international bestsellers with our books flying off the shelves. Who wouldn't?

While you can have the pie-in-the-sky dream, you also need to have a realistic plan for this month, this year, and this decade for your books. This is all to say that the plan you make needs to be specific to where you are starting now and what you know you can commit to.

Your version of "going wide" will likely not match my version of going wide. And my version of wide today will not match my wide strategy in five years.

Let me explain in a different way. Let's say there is an author with a catalog of a dozen books that are all only available through Amazon. They order forty author copies to sell at a local book fair. They're a wide author as they expanded their reach to more than one platform.

An author with a single book translated into three different languages that is available on five different online retailers with global reach, at two local bookstores, and has an e-commerce function on their website is a wide author.

They're both wide.

If you sell even one copy of your book outside the Amazon platform, you're wide! Get a pin and a sticker and wave the wide-flag. If you sell all of your books through retailers outside of the 'Zon, you're also wide.

Wide is wide. You get to decide just how wide your strategy will be. Don't let anyone tell you that you have to follow their specific plan in order to qualify as wide.

So now that we are clear that wide is any self-publishing strategy where you sell books outside of Amazon, let's go back and figure out why you weren't wide to begin with.

Why weren't you wide to begin with?

Why did you choose to only publish on Amazon? Because it was the easy option? Did you invoke the Pareto Principle (80/20)? There are so many different reasons why authors initially elect this route. Some authors just wanted to get the book out as a proof of concept. Some just to say "I did it!" If making a career out of being an author wasn't your primary goal in writing your book, you likely didn't spend months and years looking on how to publish across multiple platforms. Many of the authors I work with are business owners. They publish workbooks, memoirs, or guides that are related to their business. These books compliment their on-line courses, drive readers into their coaching funnel, or add an additional line of revenue to their business. In some cases, they aren't looking to build a book-publishing empire, they just want the book out and don't want or need the hassle of managing multiple print-on-demand publishing platforms.

Did you decide to stick with an Amazon-only strategy because they offered great incentives to stay exclusive? The pull of KU (Kindle Unlimited) dollars and the marketing options available with Kindle Select are serious. And many authors do well with these programs, especially if they publish in the right genres. But nothing good can last forever and you may have started to see those payouts decline. What worked then doesn't work now, that happens. No author should expect any strategy to work forever.

So, I'm here to say that you didn't do anything wrong. Maybe the Amazon-only strategy worked for you when you started. Maybe that was the only option you were aware of. Whatever the reasoning, you still have a book that is published and available for sale on one of the largest retailers in the world. Pat yourself on the back!

Before you embark on this journey to bring your book from one platform to many, you need to define your goals. I've seen authors rush to go wide and when the technical elements get a little hard, or the platforms get glitchy (which they all do), they get frustrated. Each platform has unique nuisances to contend with. I don't blame the authors, this isn't easy. But with a clear goal in mind, it can make the effort worth it. And it will guide you in making a plan for how to go wide.

Yes, there is more than one way to go wide, which we will dive into shortly. It isn't just one button that you press that takes your book to every other possible retailer in the world.

But first, let's really think back to why you opted to just sell on Amazon. Keep that in mind, because you may very well get to the end of this book and decide to stick with that strategy. Let's explore some of the top reasons that authors decide to go wide.

Increased opportunities for book sales

This is the main reason that many authors elect to bring their books to a larger marketplace. The more storefronts that carry your book (brick-and-mortar as well as online), the more opportunities you have to make a sale. Simply put, not everyone buys everything from Amazon. Even their biggest brand evangelist will eventually need to buy something outside of the Amazon ecosystem. Many people still enjoy perusing bookstores and letting a book find them, they enjoy picking them up and glancing at the description. Amazon is great for finding exactly what you want and while they have discoverability tools, book lovers will always enjoy the ambiance and experience of shopping for books in person.

Also, for everyone who loves Amazon, there is probably someone who doesn't. While many people swear by their excellent prices and super-speedy delivery, some people loathe to support the mega-corporation. These book lovers are shopping for books on Google, Apple, Barnes & Noble, Kobo, Walmart, Target, you name it. An Amazon-only book is never going to get in front of this group. When your book is in these other places, you increase the chances of someone making the purchase.

Increased international exposure

And that is just in the United States. For those of us who were born and raised in the good ole' U.S. of A. it is sometimes hard to remember that not everywhere else in the world is just like home. There are some countries that don't have access to Amazon, or who make better use of other online retailers. While your book may only be available in English, there are English-speaking readers all over the world that you can't reach with Amazon. If you have the specific goal of reaching a larger international audience, then your strategy for going-wide will be very different from another author who is primarily focused on increasing their domestic sales. Or, if you already have translated versions of your books available on Amazon, you may find that once your books are available on other international self-publishing platforms that your sales jump.

"I want to see my book on the shelves at a store or library"

Ah, the dream. I haven't met a single author in my life who didn't daydream about signing copies of their books in a store packed with raving fans. Unfortunately, those who elect to publish exclusively with Amazon usually have those fantasies crushed the second they tell a shop owner that their book is on Amazon.

Do you know why?

Bookstores hate Amazon! They really do!

And it is easy to see why. Many brick-and-mortar bookstores have seen their in-store sales drop because of Amazon. Not only is Amazon able to sell books at a loss to offer the lowest possible price to readers, but they have everything in stock. A local bookstore can't keep the inventory that Amazon does. And many shop owners have seen would-be customers come in, find a book they love, search for it on their phones, order it through Amazon, and then place the store's copy back on the shelf. How heart-breaking!

The fastest way to get a bookstore to refuse to stock your book is to say, "My book is available on Amazon!" You are rubbing salt in a deep wound.

Getting your book distributed through a different print-on-demand service will help make this dream a bit easier to realize, although it will still take some work. We'll go into which options best support this strategy.

It is important to remember your reasons for going wide. Each author has their own strategy, you may be halfway through this process and talk with a fellow author who is sticking with an Amazon-only strategy and start to think, "why am I doing all this work?" Remember, if it is your goal to increase your sales (domestic or international) and have more retailers carrying your book then write that down. Put it on a post-it note by your desk. Hang it on the fridge with a magnet. Your strategy is unique to you and you will have a moment when you need a reminder to help you stay the course.

Going wide doesn't mean abandoning Amazon

Most importantly, remember that self-publishing your book outside of the Amazon ecosystem doesn't mean that you are abandoning Amazon altogether. They are one of the largest online retailers in the world. As indie authors, we owe so much to Amazon for the evolution the company sparked in book selling. Without the emergence of online book buying via Amazon there never would have been the revolution in eBooks and eReaders. Without Kindle Direct Publishing (KDP) many of us would still be struggling to sell eBooks online and have them listed with retailers. Without their print-on-demand service acquired when Amazon purchased CreateSpace, many of us would not have print books because of the upfront investment of an offset run. Authors still need Amazon in their mix.

But if 2020 taught us anything, it is that massive changes can happen—quickly! While book sales soared during the quarantine, many of us lost income during the pandemic. Amazon may have thrived in the early days of lockdown, but many businesses faltered. If Amazon is our ONLY source of royalties, what happens when this mega-company does stumble? Or when they reduce royalties to authors? Or when they are forced to break apart into smaller companies? Or when any number of infinite possibilities occur?

The purpose of going wide isn't to stop selling your book on the Amazon ecosystem (Amazon.com and Audible). It is to give your readers more opportunities to find your book on their retailer of choice.

In fact, we cannot abandon Amazon. We as authors rely on this company and stand on the shoulders of what they have built. But it is Amazon who can and, in some ways, has already abandoned us. They started as an online bookstore but have now shifted their corporate focus to more lucrative lines of business. We've seen this over the years with deprioritizing book shipments, increase in ad costs, squeezes on the wholesale discount, and so much more.

So no, we are not going to turn away from Amazon altogether. But, by the time you finish reading this book you will have a solid plan to be able to make your book available through other retailers so that you can survive as an author without Amazon if you ever needed to.

But first, who are these other retailers and how can you get access to them?

PART 2

Where Do You Want
Your Books to Be?

Just how wide is the world of "wide publishing?" That is like asking, "how big is the sky?" For you as an author, wide could mean uploading your book to every possible self-publishing platform out there. (I don't recommend that.) Or wide could mean adding your book to only a few select retailers outside of the Amazon ecosystem. Wide is as big and as expansive as you would like it to be for your book.

As you read through this part of the book, I encourage you to take notes and consider each platform before you dive in. It will be tempting to get started right now. But please finish the entire book before you do so. I've seen many authors who are eager to go wide and they end up signing up for every single platform. This usually ends up with a big ole mess. Why? Because some of the aggregators distribute to the same platforms, which can create a duplicate record. That can cause a headache for you and a poor experience for your readers who will ultimately click away and buy a different book. We don't want that to happen. A little bit of planning can go a long with in this process.

I've also created a summary PDF of the platforms and I'd recommend having this pulled up alongside the subsequent chapters to see how they piece together. You can access this and the other planning PDFs for this book at **AuthorYourAmbition.com/Wide/**

No matter how excited you are to get started and sign up for everything, just pack a little patience first. After reading through this section of the book, you will be able to create a list of retailers that you want to be on, which platforms will get you there, and then come up with a step-by-step plan to execute.

As a side-note, when I review each of the self-publishing platforms, I will give you information on how the platforms handle taxes. Some will provide you with a 1099, others will not. For us authors, end of the year taxes are a blessing and a curse. A blessing, because income that we need to pay taxes on means that we sold books. Yay! But the curse comes when we have to sort through all of our platforms and figure out which ones provide what forms, what information is missing, etc. ***I'm not an accountant and I'm most certainly not your accountant***. As you weigh the pros and cons of each platform, be sure to talk with your accountant to see how these new platforms will impact your filings.

To be fair, by the time I hit "publish" on this book, there will already be new platforms entering the market. I'll do my best to keep my website and YouTube channel up to date on the latest and greatest so you can always learn more at AuthorYourAmbition.com. But, as of the time I am writing this book (July 2021), I have included the most commonly used and widely accepted industry leaders in the self-publishing space.

You may notice a few platforms are not included in this book. As I sought to get as much information as I could to you, I realized I was playing a game of whack-a-mole. As soon as I said, "yes, this list is complete," another platform would be brought to my attention. In addition to the platforms that I use, there are many more that I do not employ in my wide strategy. I could have continued to meddle with this manuscript forever, but since that helps no one, I decided to cut this list off. I will release new editions of this book from time to time with more platforms listed as the landscape changes and will keep my website and channel updated with new information as it becomes available.

Deciding which platforms to add

We'll first review the platforms where you upload your book directly with the retailer. Then, we will talk about aggregators, those easy-to-use distribution platforms that take your book and get it out across multiple retailers. Next, we will talk about how you can sell your book directly to readers and cut out the middle-men-and-women altogether. And last, we will talk about what you need to do before pitching brick-and-mortar stores as well as other marketing strategies.

This is the order of operations that I follow when I upload my books, it is reflected in how this section of the book is organized:

1. Direct Platforms
2. Aggregators
3. Website
4. Brick-and-Mortar

My personal strategy and mix of retailers and aggregators will be listed at the end of Chapter 3, once we've reviewed all the available retailer platforms. This way you can learn about each of the platforms first to understand why I have this mix and what your mix should look like distinct from my own. Please don't skip ahead to just see what I do and copy that. I may not be the best route for you and your book.

As a note about the direct versus aggregator strategy, you are going to make a better royalty when you list your book directly with the retailer in most cases. You are cutting out the middleman, the aggregator, and you don't have to give them a cut of your royalties as well. When you are pricing your eBooks at $0.99 or even $3.99, we're talking a savings of pennies. But every cent adds up when you are selling a lot of books. But the additional cost may be worth it to you so that you can have your books uploaded to a handful of platforms instead of managing a slew of logins.

Keep in mind that while you earn more with the direct platforms, you are not their customer or their priority. Their customers are the priority. While they will work hard to address any technical issues, they only added on the self-publishing direct feature to make more money, not to service your author career. The self-publishing aggregators on the other hand were built with authors in mind. You may find the tools and services on the aggregators to be more conducive to your growth.

Account set up

Before you dive in and start creating logins, please read through all of the different options in this chapter and complete the planning exercise in the next section.

Instead of discussing the set-up instructions and process for each publishing platform, I can tell you now that there are minimal differences. Every platform requires you to set up a login, create a profile, and complete your tax and bank information all before you upload your book. Most platforms allow you to drag and drop your files to upload, but the few that require you to upload by navigating to the file location aren't really that much more difficult.

Effectively, don't base your decision of where to publish on the set-up process. No one publishing platform is that onerous or simplified to make a difference in this decision.

CHAPTER 2

Retailers—Direct

There are a few online retailers that allow you to upload your book with them directly, just as you do with Amazon. It is a great one-to-one relationship. Publish with Amazon, book is for sale on Amazon. Publish with Barnes & Noble, book is for sale on the Barnes & Noble website. Easy to understand. There are four big players outside of Amazon KDP that allow this. You will also be able to get your eBooks and print books to these platforms via aggregators, which we will cover in the next chapter.

Let's start with the other tech giant in the room…Google.

Google Play

https://play.google.com/books/publish/u/0/

Pros

By listing your book directly on Google Play you have a huge potential audience. Now, not everyone who owns an Android device will necessarily access the Google Books App, like your genre of book, or think to purchase it directly from this service. But the point of being wide is that you are available to those who do. Also, when someone "Googles" your pen name or the book title, the Google Play Book Page will display in the search engine results, where a reader could buy your book. It seems silly to spell it out, but the primary advantage of being on the Google platform is this... it's Google!

One specific advantage I've found from being on this platform is that international readers from countries that don't have Amazon, can still purchase my books on Google. (Or just international readers who don't go to Amazon as their first stop for books, will go to Google.) The potential reach here is huge.

Cons

There are three main drawbacks to selling your eBooks through Google Play:

1. You have to come to the platform with a formatted ePub file. This is your responsive file that is fit to be read on an eReader device. With Amazon you can upload your MS Word document and it will convert to ePub for you, but Google doesn't do this. So that means you need to find a way to format the file prior to uploading. This would require you to use a formatting software, work with a professional formatting service, or download a copy of the formatted file from another platform.

2. You can only sell eBooks. This is a one format platform which means you are adding to your workflow without much efficiency. Also, readers who prefer physical books won't be able to purchase through Google. (You can get your Audiobook listed on the Google Play Bookstore, but you'll have to go through an aggregator.)

3. Not everyone uses this platform. While this is true of Amazon and every other platform that we will discuss in this section, it still bears mentioning. There is no one magic platform that gets you out everywhere. So don't expect that by uploading your book here that you will magically have a boat-load of book sales overnight. (Just keeping it real.)

Payout

Google provides two methods for payments: EFT (electronic funds transfer) direct to your bank account and wire transfer. For funds to post via EFT you need to have a minimum of $1.00 U.S. Dollars in royalties. These pay on the 15th of the month so long as it is not a weekend or holiday, then it will post the next business day. Wire transfers require a $100 U.S. Dollars minimum.

Formats

For the Google Play Bookstore you can only upload your eBooks. While the end user can go to the Google Play Bookstore and see both eBooks and Audiobooks for sale, you as the author can only upload the eBook file. (We will get to the Audiobooks when we discuss Findaway Voices and other Audiobook aggregators in the next chapter.)

Taxes

Google will provide a 1099 to authors at the end of the year if they have paid out over $10. This may seem like a silly little threshold. Until you realize that you uploaded your first book to the platform in November, were paid $9 in December because you didn't properly market to your audience that you were on a new platform, and then you have business income without any form. It is important to keep this in mind and add the platform to your mix early enough in the year that you will receive enough of a payout to generate a 1099. You can still report the income without a 1099, but it starts to make your taxes that much more complicated.

Can you get to this retailer via other platforms?

Yes!

As of right now, you can get your eBook onto the Google Play Bookstore directly or through one of two aggregators: PublishDrive and LuLu.

To get your Audiobooks listed in the Google Play Bookstore, you have to go through Findaway Voices or Author's Republic. This is where having a non-exclusive contract for your Audiobook with ACX is very important. (We will go over ACX Exclusivity in Chapter 6.)

Kobo

https://www.kobo.com/us/en/p/writinglife

Pros

Kobo is a truly international platform with over 12 million readers in 190 countries using their eReaders. They also support almost 70 different languages. If you are looking to reach an international audience, Kobo can get you there! For many U.S. citizens, it is hard to imagine, but there is a world outside our borders and not everyone uses Amazon. Kobo is an excellent service used by readers around the world.

The Kobo Writing Life platform also allows self-publishing authors to run and manage their own promotions and provides very clear metrics and tracking on sales. Other platforms have a ways to go in terms of providing this level of clarity with sales.

Cons

Just like with Google Play, not everyone uses Kobo or owns one of their eReaders. You are expanding your reach, but Kobo is not a cure-all solution. It is one retailer. A popular one, but not a panacea.

Payout

Once you have sold at least $50 CAD (Canadian Dollars), Kobo will pay out 45 days after the end of the month. This is known as net-45 payments.

Formats

For a long time, you could only upload your eBook to Kobo. Now you can also sell your Audiobook on this platform directly. Kobo focuses on digital books so no print options on this site, for readers or for authors.

Taxes

For U.S. based authors, do not expect to receive a 1099 at the end of the year from Kobo. You will have to keep your monthly payment reports and give those to your accountant at the end of the year.

Can you get to this retailer via other platforms?

Yes, in fact I don't go directly with Kobo. I get my books listed on their website via Smashwords for eBook and Findaway Voices for audio. When I started on my self-publishing journey, I knew I wanted wide distribution, but the idea of managing multiple logins, learning multiple platforms, and balancing writing with my day job was just a bit too much. So, I found an aggregator that could get me everywhere I wanted to be at the time and would also allow me to publish direct on Amazon.

You can get to Kobo through Smashwords, Draft2Digital, IngramSpark, and PublishDrive for eBooks and Findaway Voices and Author's Republic for Audiobooks.

Apple

https://authors.apple.com/

Pros

Raise your hand if you have an iPhone or iPad. If you live in the U.S., chances are that you do. And that means you have iTunes, iBooks, iEverything at your fingertips. For authors, the chance to have their books in the Apple Books library is a huge opportunity. The potential reach is massive.

By publishing direct with Apple, you have more control over the price, discounts, and the ability to use affiliate links when promoting your book.

Cons

Just like with the previous two direct retailers, while the reach is wide, Apple isn't a one-stop shop to sell millions of books. For starters, this platform only offers readers eBooks or Audiobooks. Just like Kobo and Google Play you are limited to digital sales only. While more readers are getting comfortable with these formats, print books are still popular.

Payout

Apple pays out monthly once you have reached a minimum of $10 U.S. Dollars in sales.

Formats

While readers can purchase eBooks or Audiobooks from Apple, authors can only upload their eBooks to the platform. You will need to get the Audiobook listed on Apple through another distributor. (We'll discuss those soon.)

Taxes

Apple will provide at 1099-K if you have more than $20,000 in unadjusted gross sales across more than 200 transactions. If you fall under that threshold, be sure to save your financial statements and give those to your accountant.

Can you get to this retailer via other platforms?

You can get to Apple through Smashwords, Draft2Digital, and PublishDrive for eBooks and Findaway Voices,

Author's Republic, and ACX for Audio. In fact, Apple seems to be the one retailer that you can get to as easily as Amazon. Given the reach of the Apple ecosystem, in the U.S. and abroad, this is an excellent opportunity for us self-publishing authors. But there are almost too many options to get here for there to be one clear path to take. Just rest assured that you will easily get your digital books onto this platform, directly or through an aggregator.

Barnes & Noble Press

https://press.barnesandnoble.com/

Pros

So many authors have looked to Barnes & Noble as the big name in bookstores for so long because, well, they have been the biggest chain bookstore for most of the past three decades. Being able to publish directly to Barnes & Noble allows you the prestige of knowing your book is for sale on their website while you are able to collect royalties on your sales.

Cons

Since B&N Press launched, I have heard about customer service issues with the platform. Uploading issues, proofs delayed, etc. In my opinion, this is because Barnes & Noble has a lot of experience and is the big name in selling books. Their foray into self-publishing is uncharted territory for the company, as such, they are learning.

Payout

B&N Press pays out monthly once you have reached a minimum of $10 U.S. Dollars in sales. They pay out on a net-30 basis, so 30 days after the month closes that amount is paid.

Formats

B&N Press allows you to self-publish eBooks as well as print books. For print you can select from paperback or hardcover options. All books are made available on the Barnes & Noble website, not necessarily in their brick-and-mortar stores.

Taxes

B&N Press will provide at 1099-MISC for active U.S. Vendors. You can enroll to receive it electronically or it can be mailed to you.

Can you get to this retailer via other platforms?

You can get to Barnes & Noble through Smashwords, Draft2Digital, and PublishDrive for eBooks, IngramSpark for print books, and Findaway Voices and Author's Republic for nook. Barnes & Noble is another retailer where you have many options to get your book on their website directly or via aggregators.

What is an aggregator you ask? We'll cover them next.

CHAPTER 3

Aggregators—Indirect

After reading through those platforms, you may start to realize that the number of logins, tax documents, and manuscripts to upload is getting pretty cumbersome. While Amazon along with Google and Apple may make up the vast majority of the U.S. eBook market, you as an author need to decide how much time and effort you have to maintain relationships with every retailer. This is where an aggregator can be a huge help. While you won't have a direct relationship with the retailer, you will save yourself time and mental bandwidth by working with an aggregator to get your books out.

My top advice for any author planning to work with an aggregator is to pick one and stick with it. I've seen authors who are eager to go wide sign up for every platform, direct and the aggregators, only to have a huge headache down the line because of duplicate listings and issues getting their books to display properly. Wide does not mean signing up with every platform, but it does mean making your book accessible to multiple retailers. After reading this section, you'll have a better idea of which aggregators would work best for your strategy.

Here are the details for each of the popular platforms:

IngramSpark

https://myaccount.ingramspark.com/

In the world of wide self-publishing, IngramSpark is one of the biggest names. With the creation of Spark, independent authors and self-publishers could finally access the massive distribution network and reach of the Ingram juggernaut. However, it comes at a price. While Ingram has curated a global and extensive network of retailers, built their printing service with Lightning Source, and continued to maintain a positive reputation within publishing, the Spark business line has not been without challenges. However, for authors who want to self-publish wide, IngramSpark has a powerful platform.

Pros

The first benefit to self-publishing with IngramSpark is that they offer hardcover books in multiple formats. You can order a case laminate (with or without a jacket) or digital cloth (with or without a jacket). Most readers are familiar with the jacket that comes on their hardcover book, the nice wrap around cover with the flaps that can double as book marks. But underneath, the author can select if they want digital cloth (a printed image of cloth binding) or the full cover wrap (case laminate) directly printed on the book. This benefit is unique to IngramSpark. Having access to self-publish hardcover books via print-on-demand means that readers have more options and makes the title more appealing to libraries who need durable books that can withstand multiple uses. (While Amazon is piloting this feature in 2021, they will still only get the book onto Amazon, not wide.) Some authors may happily report that a library purchased a copy of their book from Amazon. That is likely the exception, it is certainly not the rule. We will talk more about libraries in Chapter 5.

The next benefit of working with IngramSpark is that they are a one-stop shop for many self-publishing authors. In fact, if you value simplicity, IngramSpark may be the only platform you elect to work with outside of Amazon. Because you can get your eBook and print books out via their network, you may find that it is easiest to upload to IngramSpark and not worry about managing multiple accounts. However, if you do plan to upload directly with Barnes & Noble or Apple, do not sign those distribution agreements when you are going through the account set up. You will see those prompts when you first sign in and start populating your account information. Do not sign the agreements unless you want your book distributed with that specific retailer. If you already have distribution with them, you don't want a duplicate record.

The reach of the Ingram network is what most self-publishing authors are after. With access to OverDrive, Hoopla, Baker&Taylor, Walmart, Target, and more, your book can go very, very wide with this one platform. However, many of the other aggregators can get you to these platforms as well.

IngramSpark offers the ability to set a wholesale discount and manage returns. This opens the potential for authors to sell their books into physical bookstores. We'll go into this strategy more in Chapter 5 and why these two features are very important. But keep in mind, that if your strategy is to get into your local bookstore or even a big box chain bookstore, IngramSpark is going to be your preferred print-on-demand vendor. We will discuss the brick-and-mortar strategy more in Chapter 5, but keep in mind now that if you have any ambition to see your books on the shelves at your local store that you will need to work with IngramSpark.

Cons

Let's get the biggest negative out of the way first. Yes, you have to pay to upload or edit your manuscript on IngramSpark. After any amount of time working with Amazon where you can upload and edit for free with little to no repercussions, the idea of paying to upload can be unsettling. Especially when those fees are $25-$49 depending on the format. While IngramSpark usually supplies free upload and edit codes several times a year and there are professional associations that provide members with codes year-round (Alliance of Independent Authors and Independent Book Publishers Association), it can still frustrate many authors that they need to pay. After outsourcing editing, design, and marketing, the idea of coughing up more can be a real challenge to many authors. After all, royalties can be slim.

I try to look at this from a business perspective. Ingram wants and needs to maintain good relationships with their vendors. By putting up this pay barrier, it makes authors think twice before they hit upload. *Is this book really ready? Should I proof it one final time, just so I don't risk having to pay the change fee?* If IngramSpark can incentivize you to double or triple check before hitting upload that saves everyone (you, IngramSpark, their partners, and the readers) a lot of headaches. It is a small fee up front that can save you a lot of frustration on the back end.

Another downside to working in IngramSpark is that they pay on a net-90 basis. This is actually a fairly common payment method. I worked for years as a digital media buyer and nearly all of our contracts were net-90. This allowed time for invoices to be received, processed, and paid. In the case of IngramSpark, any book sales on a retailer website must be reported and then paid to IngramSpark before they can pay you. I often see authors complaining on forums that they are being ripped off or that IngramSpark is up to something shady because they haven't received their payments yet. The payment terms are listed plain and simple, it takes 90 days. Amazon takes at least 60, so this isn't that much longer of a wait.

For a similar reason, you'll see your sales figures updated periodically. Again, IngramSpark is an aggregator, they are not the retailer. They have to wait for the retailers to report a sale. Because of this, you're not going to see print or eBook sales reported the same day like you do on Amazon. (To be clear, most of the aggregators work this way. You won't see up-to-the-minute stats on your books.) For this reason, I look at my sales via IngramSpark once a month when they send their report.

Finally, the last detractor to working with IngramSpark is their customer service. I used to work in a customer service role, it is never easy. No one ever contacts customer service to say, "hey, you're doing a great job!" No. People only write in with problems. And when the customer is an author who has been working on their book for years, they tend to be a bit more passionate in their need to get an answer right away. I get it. From an outsider's perspective, it seems that the exponential growth on IngramSpark with the shift to wide publishing has given them more customers (and therefore more customer complaints) than they were equipped to handle. Throughout much of 2020 I noticed many posts throughout self-publishing Facebook groups with irritated authors. To be fair, I posted one of my own when I had a shipment go missing, but it was eventually resolved. I'm not making excuses for IngramSpark, as a business they should have an easy and efficient customer service team. It seems that as of mid-2021 they are making some changes to streamline the process. While they have a long way to go to improve this aspect of working with their platform, this doesn't mean that the other aggregators are any better. No one is immune to missed shipments, metadata errors, publication lags, and general technology glitches.

Payout

IngramSpark pays out on a net-90 basis, subject to returns. This means if someone buys your book and returns it, IngramSpark will include that in the report and you won't get paid for that sale. This is standard and appreciated. Returns stink, but it would be even worse if IngramSpark had paid me and then had to ask for that money back. You could try to avoid returns completely by not making your print books returnable. Personally, all of my books are returnable and I've had only a handful in the years I've been working with IngramSpark. It doesn't impact my sales enough for me to worry on it.

You can elect to be paid via a direct deposit into your checking account or via PayPal. For U.S. Dollars and British Pounds there are no minimum sales required for payments to be distributed. For Canadian Dollars, Euros, and Australian Dollars there are minimums of $25 to be met prior to distributions.

Formats

IngramSpark allows authors to publish eBooks (ePub file), paperback, and hardcover books.

Taxes

One of the most frustrating aspects of working with IngramSpark is that at the end of the year, they do not provide 1099 tax forms for U.S. authors. You can save your monthly payment reports or pull one for the entire calendar year for your taxes.

Smashwords

https://www.smashwords.com/

For those of us who have been self-publishing for a few years now, Smashwords used to be one of a few aggregators back in the day. Now newer platforms are in the mix. While these new platforms can offer the same thing, many wide authors have continued to stick with Smashwords. For me, it is easier to keep my wide eBook distribution through Smashwords than to remove all of my books from this platform and their vendors and add them again somewhere else.

Pros

The biggest reason that I use Smashwords is their distribution network. This is the main benefit to uploading your eBook to Smashwords. Your eBook will be listed with the Smashwords Premium Catalog that includes Barnes &

Noble, Apple, Kobo, OverDrive, Hoopla, Baker&Taylor, and Gardners.

Smashwords has their own eBook storefront. When you upload your eBook to Smashwords it will be included in this listing. However, you need to pass their rigorous series of checks in order to be included in the Premium Catalog (i.e., get your book out to the retailers.) When you upload your eBook, Smashwords will automatically do this check for you.

The AutoVetter system evaluates your eBook file for any errors. This is super helpful to ensure that your book is accepted and provides a good reading experience for your audience. If any issues are caught, you will receive an email detailing the corrections that need to be made before the book can be accepted. You'll also see this designation on your dashboard when you log into Smashwords as well. The AutoVetter has assisted in catching formatting, spacing, and graphics issues in my uploads, so this is an added benefit to Smashwords.

Cons

The first drawback to Smashwords is in their 1.0 look and feel. The website doesn't look sleek or fancy, but you don't need it to look well-designed, you just need it to work. Smashwords does have a bookstore where your book will be listed for sale, but I find the biggest benefit is their distribution network. If I was worried about getting sales from the Smashwords bookstore, I would be concerned about how the website looks. But that isn't the case, so I don't sweat it too much.

The AutoVetter can sometimes be a little too sensitive. As an example, one of my books was held back from their Premium Catalog for further review because it thought I didn't put my name as the publisher on the copyright page. My name was there as it always is, no variation from the other manuscripts I had uploaded previously. It was resolved and got through the system, but it was a little concerning to get an email saying it was rejected and would have to be submitted for a manual review.

Just as with Google, Smashwords only sells digital versions of your book. While you can link to your print and Audiobook formats from your Smashwords book page, you still have to find another platform to sell those versions from. When you sign on with Smashwords you are getting eBook distribution and that's it. So, it can be a lot of work for just one format, however the reach of their distribution network is an excellent resource.

Payout

You can elect for a check to be mailed once you reach a minimum payment threshold of $75. Or you can elect to receive payments via PayPal without the payment threshold.

Formats

Smashwords is a digital aggregator and does not provide print-on-demand services for print books. You can add links to where your Audiobook is sold, but you cannot upload your audio files for distribution through this aggregator. In 2018, Smashwords entered into an agreement with Findaway Voices for wide Audiobook distribution so that you can upload your eBook to Smashwords and submit your title to Findaway Voices.

Taxes

At the end of the year Smashwords does send a 1099 for U.S. income tax purposes.

StreetLib

https://www.streetlib.com/

While many of the direct self-publishing platforms and the other aggregators already mentioned will get you to some of the largest markets in the world, they cannot get you everywhere. Even Amazon isn't in every country and the other platforms mentioned to date have holes in their global network. StreetLib offers a truly global reach with retailers in Africa, the Middle East, and Asia, as well as the Americas, Europe, and Oceania. Effectively, they have retailers in every continent except Antarctica. While you may not anticipate that your book will sell well in other countries if it is not translated into the local language (which is certainly a factor), you can still sell the English-language version of your book globally.

Pros

The main benefit to StreetLib is their truly global reach. While I have access to many of these retailers through other aggregators, there are some that I simply cannot get to without StreetLib. And since the aggregators available to me as a resident of the U.S. are not available to all authors around the world, StreetLib is an excellent aggregator for self-publishing authors in countries and regions not currently served by the major platforms.

If your version of going wide means getting your book out to the "whole wide world," StreetLib is an excellent option. You will be able to list your book with retailers throughout the world. Just be sure to de-select the retailers you already have access to via direct platforms or other aggregators when uploading.

Cons

While the sales dashboard is very slick and appealing, the upload center and process are a little clunky. If you already have your files, you need to go straight to upload, not "create." That section will have you reuploading your MS Word file to generate a new ePub document. (Remember, even if you create your manuscript as a Google Doc, you will need to download it as a MS Word Doc and save it as the 1997-03 .doc version, not .docx.) If you already have that file, you'll waste time and get really frustrated. (Although, if you don't have an ePub file you can use their creator service.)

I've also noticed that each time I upload a file and complete the metadata, the book is listed in grey as "invalid" or in red with errors. My immediate reaction is to go back in and fix something. What I have now learned is that the system shows this for all uploads. Take a minute and then refresh the page. If the book isn't displaying in green with no errors, then go back in to correct. The system just needs a moment to update.

While there is no upfront fee to list on StreetLib and therefore very little downside to self-publishing with them, I will also say that the upside can be small as well. If you aren't going to advertise or promote your books in these other countries, don't expect a surge of sales. You'll need to build your audience in these regions, just like you have to build them at home. If your books aren't translated, you are limiting your reach in new countries to those who want to read in your language. But those readers do exist.

Payout

StreetLib pays on a net-60 basis. (This means you get paid 60 days after the sale is reported). You can do a direct transfer to a bank account or your PayPal account.

StreetLib is a registered corporation out of Italy. On the StreetLib website you will first see details for payouts in euros. You will need to click over to their article that is specific to the U.S. and Canada. For those of us who live and write in the U.S. or Canada, any payout will be made from their subsidiary in North America. If you select a direct deposit to your bank, there is a $20 minimum threshold and for PayPal a $10 minimum.

Formats

StreetLib allows authors to self-publish eBooks, print-on-demand paperbacks, and Audiobooks.

Taxes

StreetLib does provide 1099 to U.S. based authors for their end-of-year tax forms.

Draft2Digital (D2D)

https://www.draft2digital.com/

This is a platform that I don't have any personal experience with. That's right, I'm a wide-author and I don't use every platform out there. Why? Because I can get access to almost all of the platforms available through Draft2Digital (D2D) through Smashwords. This is why it is important to not just sign up for every single platform. It would not only waste my time, but it would likely cause a lot of headaches if I used both aggregators for my eBooks. So, I don't do that.

Depending on which aggregator you like the best, you may elect to use D2D over Smashwords for your eBooks.

Or maybe for ease of use, you'll just go with IngramSpark for everything. The only wrong option among these aggregators is signing up for every single one. Pick the platform that suits you the best and go with that one.

Pros

The first benefit that appeals to many authors is that you can convert your manuscript to ePub and print with Draft2Digital. With other aggregators you either need to bring completed files or there is a charge to convert them. For authors who don't have the funds yet to invest in formatting software or to hire a designer, this is a great option. Most aggregators and direct platforms have an eBook conversion option, but most don't have one for print formatting. This feature is unique to D2D.

Once your book is ready to sell you can make use of the Books2Read function within the platform. This allows you to create a Universal Book Link. Now that your book is available outside of the Amazon ecosystem, you'll have lots of options for readers to purchase your book. Instead of providing them with a dozen unique links, you can use this one page to allow them to pick their preferred retailer to find your book. We'll go into this strategy more in Part 3. You can create a page like this on your own website as well, but Books2Read will remember a reader's preferred retailer which will save them time when they are eager to find and purchase your book.

The next benefit is especially helpful to those who work with other authors to cowrite. Draft2Digitlal is one of a few aggregators that allows for collaborator payments. This means that if you and another author cowrote a book, D2D will automatically send you the correct royalty. This is much easier and cleaner than one of you receiving the royalty and invoicing each other for the portion due.

Through this network you will have access to the major retailers as well as the big library networks OverDrive, Hoopla, and Baker&Taylor. The only difference I can spot in the distribution between Draft2Digital and the other aggregators at the time of this writing is that Vivlio is in their network and when you distribute to Kobo you can still access the Kobo Plus subscription-based reading service.

You can opt to distribute to Barnes&Noble, Apple, and Kobo through Draft2Digital or you can distribute with those platforms directly. You'll just need to "unselect" them when you are setting up your book for distribution.

Cons

As I researched Draft2Digital for this book, I realized that all I had ever heard about them was very positive. This is excellent, but in 2021 it seems almost unrealistic for any company, let alone one that has any sort of technology involved, to have a spotless record. So, I did a little digging. Not trying to incite a rant thread, I asked other self-publishers what their experience was with the platform.

Were there any negatives to working with this platform? It can't be perfect.

The many happy users of this platform only reported a few niche detractors. But, since you may write in one of those niches, it should be considered when you evaluate the platform.

Some books you cannot publish through Draft2Digital:

- Erotica
- Books in the public domain
- Books with a single name author (as in Prince, Madonna, or Sting. Not just 1990s chart-toppers, one name artists)

From my research, these titles weren't banned from the site, but authors had issued with these books not going through when they tried to publish or found they were removed from the catalog after some recent changes. In each instance, they reported that they were able to get their eBook out through Smashwords.

Payout

Draft2Digital pays out royalties monthly on a net-30 basis. You can elect to have payments deposited directly to your bank account or use a digital payment system like PayPal or Payoneer. You can even request a check be mailed to you for deposit. Each method has a different payout threshold to reach before the money is sent, be sure to check the latest requirements when you are signing up.

Formats

Draft2Digital allows you to self-publish in eBook and paperback to their partner network.

Taxes

Draft2Digital provides 1099 tax forms to authors at the end of the year regardless of the number of sales made or income paid out to the author.

PublishDrive

https://publishdrive.com/

This is yet another aggregator for self-publishing your book. Yes, there are quite a few to choose from. I don't use this one (for the same reason I don't use D2D). But after reading through this section and learning more about the platform you may decide this is the best one for you and your book. While the distribution network appears to be much the same as the other aggregators, there are a few distinctions with this platform.

Pros

In addition to offering distribution to the large players in the English-speaking world, PublishDrive also has print-on-demand services in Chinese Markets. This is a distinct advantage that I have not seen other aggregators offer.

Just like Draft2Digital, PublishDrive also offers team payments with collaborators. This really does help those who work with multiple collaborators on different projects.

Another distinct benefit to working with PublishDrive is that you can access Amazon Advertising. Typically, you have to list your book with KDP in order to have access to this feature. If you are looking for one platform to manage all of your retailers, this gives PublishDrive an advantage over the others.

Cons

The main detractor with PublishDrive is that all of their plans require a monthly payment. If you sell enough books each month to cover this cost and then some, great. If not, this might be a break breaker for some authors. Even the lowest tier option for two titles is $9.99/month. If you already have more than two books out that you want to take wide, you have to go to the $19.99/month plan or higher.

Payout

PublishDrive pays authors on a net-60 basis and offers check, direct deposit, and digital payments. There is a calculator on their website so that you can check the potential fees and payout thresholds depending on the payment method.

Formats

PublishDrive offers authors the ability to self-publish your eBook, print book, or Audiobook.

Taxes

There are multiple options to fill out the tax form needed based on your country of origin. They do not withhold taxes for U.S. citizens

U.S. citizens will receive a 1099 in January for year-end tax purposes.

LuLu

https://www.lulu.com/

LuLu is our final aggregator that focuses on print and eBooks. LuLu primarily serves authors looking for print options for their books. They offer eBook publishing and distribution, but it appears to be a smaller focus. In addition to books, creators can also leverage LuLu for calendars, yearbooks, magazines, and comic books.

Pros

One thing that LuLu can offer that other aggregators do not is a wider variety of print book options. For example, you can have your books spiral bound and select a thicker paper bond than most of the print-on-demand services offer. This may seem really niche, but if you plan to offer coloring books or activity books, these distinctions can really improve the end-user experience.

Cons

A quick search may reveal a lot of negative reviews. LuLu had their fair share of customer service issues in 2020 after a new website rollout. They appear to have resolved these issues by now, but those negative comments stick around for a while on the internet.

Also, it appears that where they have better paper quality and binding options, they do cost a bit more for print-on-demand books than their competitors. However, some authors may find the additional cost for their full color children's books is warranted to ensure the colors do not bleed.

Payout

You can elect to be paid via PayPal or a check and, like some of the other aggregators, you can split payments with other contributors. There are certain thresholds to meet depending on the payment option you select, a minimum of $5 for PayPal or $20 for check. If you are below the minimum, the amount will roll over to the following pay period. For PayPal, royalties are paid monthly. For check, quarterly.

Formats

LuLu offers print-on-demand and eBooks for distribution.

Taxes

U.S. Citizens are issued a 1099 by January 31st and international authors are issued their 1042S by March 31st.

Findaway Voices

https://findawayvoices.com/

While some of the other direct platforms and aggregators already mentioned can also help you distribute your Audiobook, there are a couple of aggregators that focus specifically on Audiobooks. ACX, Audiobook Creation Exchange, which is owned by Amazon is also an Audiobook aggregator since they publish to Amazon, Audible, and Apple. However, for many authors looking to go wide, just having access to those three platforms isn't wide enough for them. Findaway Voices has distribution to over 40 retailers and growing, and includes access to public libraries.

They can also get you on to Audible and Amazon, however I recommend using both ACX and Findaway Voices. To do this you will just need to exclude Audible and Amazon from your distribution agreement with Findaway.

Pros

The first advantage to working with Findaway Voices, aside from their wide reach, is that you actually get to set the price for your Audiobook. With ACX, you don't have that option. Being able to set your price is critical for leveraging any marketing promotions (ex. discounts and sales). It is also necessary to appeal to libraries who either pay on a per download basis or purchase a license to distribute the audio files to their patrons.

After using both Findaway Voices and ACX, I also find that the upload process is much easier with Findaway Voices. I have narrated and recorded my own Audiobooks and I have had fewer issues with the upload system. Also, ACX tends to take much longer to turn around their quality assessment (QA) of the files. For my latest Audiobook that I uploaded to Findaway Voices, the book was approved and displaying with retailers within 48 hours.

Cons

One method for selling your Audiobook that Findaway Voices advertises is the ability to sell direct to consumers via Author's Direct. However, you have to pay a $99 set up fee to Author's Direct to store your files and keep your storefront going. I find that this can be prohibitive for authors who have already invested a lot of money in the narration and sound mixing and are looking at how much they would need to earn on each sale to just break even. You may be thinking that this isn't too big of a deal, since your focus may be on selling through trusted retailers. However, it impacts the number of free audio codes you can give out to try to generate reviews. Users who don't have the Author's Direct storefront can only get 30 free codes to send out, but those with the subscription get up to 100. In terms of sending out free codes to reviewers, that is a massive difference.

The next negative is sort of a common-sense item. While Findaway Voices can get your Audiobook out to a lot of retailers, it cannot get you absolutely everywhere. In this sense, wide does not mean omni-present.

Payout

Findaway Voices pays out of a net-30 basis. However, some retailers report the sales later so you will get paid a catch-up payment when they post.

Formats

Audio! That's what they do. This is one of two Audiobook aggregators outside of the Amazon ecosystem that I will review in this book and it is the one that I use for my own Audiobooks.

Taxes

At the end of the year Findaway Voices provides a 1099 for U.S. authors.

Author's Republic

https://www.authorsrepublic.com/

Author's Republic functions in much the same manner as Findaway Voices in that they allow you to self-publish your Audiobook and distribute it to many different platforms.

Pros

This platform offers the same easy-to-upload and distribute platform that Findaway Voices has. The one benefit that I can see over Findaway Voices is that Author's Republic distributes to Spotify. This is a very popular audio platform and could be a big opportunity for your Audiobook.

Cons

No ability to find a narrator to work with on their site. Both ACX and Findaway Voices offer this service to authors looking to format their books for audio. That means you need to come to the platform with finished files. If you don't have the equipment, patience, or prerogative to narrate the book yourself, you'll also have to find a narrator on your own.

Payout

Author's Republic only makes payments via PayPal once you have reached a $10 minimum threshold. They pay net-30 from when the retailers remit payment to Author's Republic.

Formats

Audio! That's what they do.

Taxes

They provide a 1099 to U.S. authors and a 1042 to those who complete the W8-BEN and W8-BEN-E forms.

My Retailer and Aggregator Mix

Now that we have covered the big players and platforms, here is my mix:

Direct Retailers:

1. Amazon KDP
2. Google Play

Aggregators:

1. Smashwords (DIGITAL ONLY)
2. ACX
3. IngramSpark
4. Findaway Voices
5. StreetLib

I've listed them in the order that I added them to my strategy. When I began self-publishing in 2015, I couldn't find information about all the options available to me in one place. I was focusing on an eBook only strategy at the time. I knew I wanted my books in libraries and Smashwords had me covered in that regard. I also knew that I needed to be on Amazon KDP as well. Those were my two platforms for the first couple of years.

Then I decided to add print into the mix in 2017. Thankfully, KDP had expanded to offer print-on-demand at that time. I still hadn't discovered IngramSpark. That year I also added Google Play into my mix. In early 2018 I decided to expand into audio and signed on with ACX. My first two Audiobooks were exclusive to that platform. At the time, audio was a bit of a gamble for me. It would be expensive and my books weren't bringing in very much. I wanted to try audio as a proof of concept first. Once I saw the success of my Audiobooks and realized the error of my ways in selecting the exclusive option, I signed on to Findaway Voices for my subsequent Audiobooks.

Finally, in 2019 I discovered IngramSpark. I listed all of my print books with the service and saw amazing growth in my sales. That same year I also discovered StreetLib, which has had mixed results.

I grew my platform mix organically over time based on what I needed in that moment. I think if I had added all seven platforms on day one, I would have been completely overwhelmed.

If I had to start all over today, I would still sign on with Smashwords and Amazon KDP first. Even though Smashwords has a very 1.0 look and feel, I like their service and their AutoVetter. I might be persuaded to try Draft2Digital instead, but I feel a sense of loyalty to Smashwords. Starting out fresh, I would sign on with IngramSpark sooner to get my print distribution set up right away. I would also likely not sign on with StreetLib again until I had translated books in my catalog. I added this platform to increase my international sales and exposure.

But to this day the majority of my international sales come from Google Play, not StreetLib.

As you can see, my strategy has evolved over time to meet the needs of my author business. You can and should as well. Pick what works for you today and go with that. Keep an eye on how you might want to expand over time, but now that you are a wide author, you will have much more freedom to add to and adapt your strategy than when you were an Amazon-only author.

As you can see there are many options for you and we haven't event touched the most important one yet: cutting out the middle-men altogether and selling direct to your readers.

CHAPTER 4

Sell Direct to Consumers

The last "platform" we'll discuss is the most important and that is—your platform. That's right, you can be your own self-publishing platform. Back in the dark days of self-publishing, before Amazon KDP opened up the flood gates, this was the only option for those brave authors who decided to go it on their own. As an author you would have to warehouse your books, host the digital files on your own website, and manage each transaction. With the dawn of self-publishing by Amazon, many authors abandoned this method for the ease of publishing on the largest on-line store.

But for the ultimate control over your creative work, you can sell it yourself. The tools available to you now are much more sophisticated than those of the early 2000s. And with your freedom to be able to sell your book anywhere, the ultimate benefit to you as an author is selling your book directly to readers. Not only do you keep the lion share of the royalties, but you can create a direct relationship with your audience. While we all dream of reaching best-seller status and having thousands, if not, millions of raving fans, the reality is that most of us will garner a modest following of superfans. Getting to connect with your readers directly is the best way to build this loyal army of readers.

Here are some of the ins and outs of selling your book directly to your customer:

Platforms To Sell Direct

So here is where words are difficult. There is this overarching concept of your author platform which covers your entire web presence as well as how you show up for your readers in person and in writing. That is your macro-concept.

Then there are the websites that service your publishing, distribution, online sales, etc. Those are also called platforms. This is your micro-concept.

In this section we are going to go over the platforms (micro-concept) that you can use to sell your book directly to your readers. These are different websites or web-service providers that make it easy for small business owners like us to sell our products directly. (Yes, as an author you are running a small, or not so small, business!)

The first platform will be your website. That's right, your website can become an ecommerce stop for readers to purchase your books directly from you. Most WYSIWYG (what-you-see-is-what-you-get) website building services offer a free version with basic blog and page building functionality. If you elect to sell your books directly on your website, you will likely need to upgrade to a paid subscription in order to integrate point-of-sale transactions and the added space for storing your ePub, Mobi, or PDF files on the web server. That was a lot of jargon and web-speak. Some of you may get that all right away. If you don't, here is a quick breakdown:

WYSIWYG website building services: this is Wordpress, Wix, Squarespace, and the like. There are dozens of services out there and they all pretty much offer the same thing. Easy to use, out of the box website templates and web page editing that anyone can figure out. The page editors look like Microsoft Word screens and you can drag and drop images at will. For more advanced designs, premium themes, and other services they usually require you to upgrade to a higher level of service.

Point-of-sale transaction: this is the way a reader can click "buy now" on your site and they can provide their payment information in a secure manner. Once the transaction is complete, they will be able to download the file (eBook or Audiobook) or you will email it to them along with their receipt. Or you could utilize both methods available for your reader so that the file doesn't get lost. It is important to remember that all customers want to ensure that their payment information is safe and secure online. Pretty much everyone has at least one horror story of finding mysterious charges on their credit card or money missing from their digital wallet. While companies make it easy to report this and replace the funds, it is still scary and a headache for customers. You want to make sure you are using secure payment services on your website. PayPal is an example of a service you can integrate to take payments on your website.

If all that tech-speak and jargon is making your head spin, I don't blame you. You may also see the cost of selling these books directly on your website start to tally up quickly, and you haven't even sold a single book outside the Amazon ecosystem yet. Here are two ways to look at this:

1. You are re-investing the royalties earned from book sales on Amazon (and other platforms) to upgrade the reader experience and appeal to a wider audience by offering the books directly on your website. It's true what they say, it takes money to make money. But it can still be daunting to look at the minimum monthly charges and think, "huh, I have to sell at least X many books a month from my website to make this worth the investment." However, this is a calculation worth running. Then you will know how much it will cost to get this up and running. You can also look at the potential time it will take as well, your time isn't cheap!

> Web server space: the reason those website building services are free is that most people who have a website need a teeny-tiny amount of space to run their website. A few pages with a couple thousand words of text each, some photos here and there, not a lot of web space being taken up. But your responsive book files and high-resolution book cover images can take up a lot of space. (Responsive files such as ePub or Mobi that automatically adjust to the screen size the reader is using.) Especially if you have a large catalog to move over. Couple that with the plug in for payments and your website is taking up a lot more room on the Wordpress (or Wix or Squarespace) servers. It's time to start paying rent.

2. Instead of getting a super tricked out website right now, you can have that as a long-term goal and find another service provider where you can sell your book and retain 95% of the royalties.

Yes, such platforms do exist. And you may be thinking, well that isn't direct from me. But it is as close as the reader can get to purchasing directly from you without having to hire a developer to make your website a savvy ecommerce retailer.

The platform I use for this function is PayHip. I can upload my eBook and Audiobook files and sell them directly. I can also create promotional codes, offer discounts and upsells, and I only lose a small percentage from each sale. I still come out far ahead in terms of royalties than when I sell through a big-name online retailer.

The upsell option is great. For example, when a reader adds *How To Write Your First Novel* to their cart, a message pops up that tells them they can save 20% off *Self-Publishing for the First-Time Author* if they purchase it now. This is great for the reader and me. And I didn't have to code a single thing!

I'm also able to integrate PayHip with my email service provider so that readers who buy a book can join my email newsletter. That means I can tell them when new books come out and have additional opportunities to connect with my fan base. This is something I have no control over when I make a sale on Amazon, Barnes & Noble, Walmart, etc.

The downside to PayHip is that they don't provide a 1099 at the end of the year for tax purposes. There is also no opportunity to leave a verified review for the book on the large retail platforms, but my audience can still rate and review on Goodreads.

Book Fairs

If the web method is not your style, not to worry. You can sell your book direct to readers the old-fashioned way: in person, at an event. While 2020 saw these events cancelled, I have no doubt that book festivals, book fairs, local author events at libraries, and in-person readings will be back. There is something special about perusing a weekend market and stopping to chat with an author while getting an autographed copy of their book. I don't think readers will stop enjoying that experience.

Finding these events in your area should be relatively easy. Try just a basic online search for "YOUR TOWN + Book Fair" and see what pops up. You can also check Facebook for events in your area too. You may want to expand your search to local weekend markets for artisans of all stripes. There, you will be one of a few authors present instead of one of a hundred at a big book fair. Not everyone at a weekend market may be looking for a book or even like your genre, but you can stand out and befriend other creatives.

One thing to keep in mind at book fairs is that your table presentation is what will draw people in. You don't need to go crazy buying professionally printed signs and banners. First of all, you will have to lug those in and out and handle set up. Secondly, the cost could be pretty high. A nice table cloth, a friendly smile, and a neat pile of books with at least one copy facing out should do.

You'll also need a method to take payments. Good ole fashioned cash is still king. Be sure to bring change so you can easily take a larger bill or denomination if that is all the customer has on hand. But we live in an increasingly cash-less society, so you will also want to have a point-of-sale option to be able to take credit cards or digital payment. I find that Stripe is the easiest to set up and use. You just need the app on your phone and a card reader. I found that when I signed up for my Stripe account, I was retargeted with an ad for a free card reader within 24 hours. I used the promo code and got my card reader for free. You'll need to remember to bring your fully charged phone with the app, your card reader, and a WiFi hot spot (or use the WiFi provided by the venue) to use this software.

In general, book fairs may be a losing proposition for you financially. Not only do you need to keep an inventory of books to sell, but many local book fairs charge a table fee. Some even charge fees to use their specific table cloth or cover so that they all look uniform. Then you will want to have some extras like bookmarks to hand out. I also like to have cookies or candy, because let's be honest, free food is a major draw for people. After all those costs, you may have to sell more books than you can carry in to break even. If foot traffic is lower than expected, you may be lugging every single copy of your book back out to the car.

Instead, think of these events as an investment. You are meeting readers face-to-face and giving them a reason to root for you and your books. Be sure to have a way for them to subscribe to your newsletter so you can keep in touch. That way this isn't a one-time interaction with a reader, but the beginning of a superfan relationship.

A bonus pro-tip for these events: bring a friend. Not only can they help you keep the line moving if you find that there are a dozen or so rabid readers at your table, but they can help you pass the time when the foot traffic is slow. Just be sure to not stay so engrossed in conversation that you turn potential customers away.

Considerations For Direct Sales

While I've already gone into the biggest consideration for these direct-to-consumer options, namely the cost, there are other elements to consider. Let's review each of them:

For digital direct-to-reader book sales, you have one big scary menacing potential outcome: someone could take your ePub file and publish it as their own. Or they could take your zip file of Audiobook chapters and resell it. Yikes! Piracy is real and at some point, we may all fall victim to it. But what if we created the monster ourselves? With every potential solution to foil book-pirates, there will inevitably be a new method for them to steal. Where there is a will, there is way. But there are some things that you can do to mitigate this.

The first is limiting the number of times a buyer can download the file. Maybe they download it to their smart phone and then said phone ends up at the bottom of a swimming pool. You want them to be able to still read the book that they purchased. Having a five download maximum should cover for regular use and user-error in downloading and accessing files. More than that and you may start to think they are sending out the link to their friends. I have this limit set within PayHip and I would recommend that you do the same. Other services allow for you to do a digital watermark on your ePub file (something I also take advantage of).

The next thing you will need to figure out when selling copies of your book is sales tax. Yep, icky annoying sales tax. But it's a fact of life. One of the things that I like the most about the majority of self-publishing platforms is that they handle the sales tax for me. I don't have to think about it. I still have to report my income earned from royalties at the end of the year for income taxes, but I don't have to remit any payments to the state or city where the book was purchased from or shipped to or warehoused in. When you sell your own books directly, you have to think about that. Especially if you are making in-person sales at a fair.

Some payment systems like Stripe will allow you to input the sales tax for the city you are in to collect that. But it is still on you to remit that payment. You also need to confirm if you owe tax to the city or the state or both. What a big pile of work.

That is why I recommend that you talk to an accountant. At this point, your business is growing more and more complex. You should speak with someone who can give you up-to-date advice about your business, your sales, and the taxes due. **I'm not your accountant**. I don't know the specific requirements for your city, state, or even country when it comes to taxes. So, talk to a professional. It doesn't have to be an onerous step before you do any direct sales, but as you start to build out your plan have a conversation. If a book fair pops up on the schedule or they have a last-minute cancellation, take advantage of the opportunity! But be sure to keep track of all your expenses and sales and bring those with you to the next meeting with your accountant.

Now that we have mitigated book thieves and taxes, let's dive into the exciting world of shipping. I know, you're reading this real page-turner of a chapter right before bed. How can you possibly stay awake through the riveting topic of processing shipments?

Well, wake up! Because this is the fun part and there are savings to be had. Finally, some good news on the topic of direct sales.

The best part of selling your printed books direct to readers is getting to autograph them. Everyone I know who has authored a book or dreamed of doing so has envisioned themselves signing copies of their book at one point or another. It is thrilling and exciting. Someone will have an autographed copy of YOUR book.

But the whole point of selling these books directly was to… you know… make at least the same royalties if not more than you would selling them online. After ordering your inventory of books, setting up your online sales system, and shipping, how much will even be left? Books are heavy, shipping has got to be crazy expensive.

Well, for authors based in the United States you can actually save big on your shipping through the United States Postal Service (USPS). They offer a program known as Media Mail. This program offers discounted shipping rates to those sending educational materials like books, DVDs, CDs, and printed music. Your book qualifies! The only exception they make on books are comic books. (Sorry, I don't make the rules.) The important thing to remember here is that this is for shipping educational materials, not promotional materials. So that means no thank you notes, bookmarks, stickers, promotional cards, etc. in the package. Just the book. Package it as you see fit. You can go into your local post office and tell the postal worker behind the counter that it is Media Mail. Or you can buy and print your postage online through Stamps.com. Either method will get you the correct rate. Just keep in mind that by using this program you agree that your package is subject to inspection to make sure you are following the rules. But that's it. Super inexpensive and easy. Finally, a savings for us small business owners.

Now whether you pass along the cost of shipping to your readers is entirely up to you. But I would recommend against it. Let's say your reader has Amazon Prime and will be able to get free shipping on the book if they order from Amazon. com. Why should they pay more to get a copy from you after shipping is included in? Yes, it will be autographed, but is that worth the extra cost? Maybe, maybe not. But if you can keep the cost the same, you are now making your offer of a signed copy that much more appealing.

Given everything I've mentioned in this section, I hope that you find the best way to sell directly to your readers. I have many of these things set up, but only a very small fraction of my sales come from this method. In some ways, I am grateful for that because I don't enjoy the added work to ship and handle taxes. But, when I get to create a better relationship with my readers, I know it is worth the added effort for those few sales.

CHAPTER 5

Selling to Brick-and-Mortar

Every author imagines the day they will see their books on the shelves. And no, not just the bookshelf in their mom's living room. But out on the world. In stores. At the library. Available for a curious reader to stumble upon it and have their minds changed forever.

Yes, the dream is intoxicating. And in this chapter, we will talk about the reality. Not only will we cover the important elements that brick-and-mortar bookstores look for, but also what libraries will require. Both strategies can be important to your version of wide, or perhaps you have no interest in either. Going wide will be the first step in giving the option to even consider these strategies.

Bookstores

One of the shared dreams that many of us authors have is to see our books on the shelves at a store. We all dream of finding our book on the front table of "best sellers", reading a section from our latest release before an autograph session, or just popping in to find our title nestled next to our favorite authors.

But this dream is often crushed for many Amazon-only authors. Why? Brick-and-mortar stores have an arch nemesis: Amazon.

The good news is that depending on which platform you select to distribute your print books, this dream could become a reality. Let's first look at what brick-and-mortar bookstores want to see when they consider stocking a book and then we will go over how you can appeal to them.

What Bookstores Want

First and foremost, stores exist to make a profit. Even the most altruistic local mom-and-pop bookstore that is all about supporting local artists and donating to children's programs still has to turn a profit. Without revenue, the store has to close up and then they can't help anyone.

There are several elements that you can control that will help make your book more appealing and profitable to bookstores:

SHIPPING PD BY RETAILER

1. Retail discount or wholesale discount
2. Pricing on book
3. Foot traffic
4. Returnable books

The first element to implement is your wholesale discount. This is something that Amazon-only authors likely haven't heard of before because KDP does not offer you the opportunity to set this. The retail price for your book is the price that you set for consumers. The wholesale discount is the price that bookstores pay for the book.

TYPO

Let's look at an example where you have priced your paperback at $14.99. That is what a reader will pay for this book. If a store were to buy your book at this price and then sell it to a consumer at the same price, they literally make nothing. If fact, they actually lose money because they had to pay shipping, sales tax, and overhead to process the shipment, get it on the shelves, and complete the transaction. This is why bookstores look for a retail or wholesale discount. They need to purchase the book at a lower price point so they can make something from the sale.

One best practice in setting your wholesale discount is to provide 55% off. That's right, more than half! It seems like a lot, but when you put yourself in the shop owner's position, they need to increase their margin in order to make ends meet. That means of the $14.99 you want to charge for the book, the store is paying you $6.74 per book. You can try to set your wholesale discount lower to increase your margin, but you will have to come to the bookstore with a compelling reason as to why they should pay a higher percentage for your book over the other titles requesting space on their shelves.

When you are setting the price for your book, you'll want to keep this discount in mind if you plan to market your book to brick-and-mortar stores. Here are the steps to take for researching your price:

1. Look at the listed retail price for books in your genre. The list price is the original price. If the book is currently on a discount, you'll want to look at the original price. Get a feel for the average price of books in your genre. You may decide that you want to price your book competitively and come in just below the average, or perhaps you want to be in the middle of the pack. I suggest running the numbers both ways to make sure you can turn a profit at either price point.
2. Once you know the price you would like to charge, run a calculator to see how much it will cost to print your book. You have to at least cover this cost with each sale, otherwise you will end up owing money.
3. Once you have number 2 (the print cost) you need to subtract that from number 1 (your list price) and then divide by number 1. This will get you the maximum percentage discount you can afford to offer.

Let's look at an example:

Let's say I decide to charge that $14.99 for my list price. After running a calculator with my print-on-demand publishing distributor, it will cost $3.75 to print my paperback (shipping has not been included in this cost yet). That means I can afford to lose up to 75% on each sale and just break even.

$$(\$14.99-\$3.75)/\$14.99 = 75\%$$

MAKING $3 PER BOOK IF 55% DISC

That is good news if I plan to offer a 55% wholesale discount and even better news if I plan to only offer a 30% discount.

So how can you even find out what your print cost is going to be? Well, the good news is that IngramSpark offers this exact calculator for you. (See the link in the resources section at the end of this book.) Note that if you plan to pursue a brick-and-mortar bookstore strategy, IngramSpark is the print-on-demand aggregator you need to select.

You can adjust your list price and retail discount and refresh the calculator to see just how much you will take home after each sale. At this time, you can only set one wholesale discount. Unfortunately, you can't offer one discount to a given vendor and a different discount to another. But you can adjust your wholesale discount at any time. Perhaps right now you don't even have the mental bandwidth to take on a brick-and-mortar retail strategy, you can set the discount low and perhaps get some surprise sales. When you are ready to focus on brick-and-mortar sales you can adjust. Just make sure your retail price works on both ends of the discount spectrum.

That part is very important as we get into the second thing that bookstores are looking for: the price on your barcode.

Yes, that is right. The clerk behind the desk or the shop manager wants to see that you have a printed price on the back of your book. This price is usually displayed on your barcode. (We are going to go into more detail on how to obtain barcodes in Chapter 7.) The bookstore will check your books into inventory when they make their purchase and log the price in their system. But, let's say the books have moved a little slowly, or perhaps they are running a special sale on your genre. They can slap a new sticker on the back of the book with a discounted price. But those systems aren't perfect. The person behind the counter may need to run the math on the discount. If your price isn't on the back of the book, it will make an already difficult situation that much more frustrating for everyone involved. The price needs to be on the book. I've heard anecdotally from authors whose local bookstore didn't have this requirement. That is great for them, but do not assume this will be the case for your local bookstore. Plan ahead and have the price on your barcode. You don't want to lose a sale (for you and the shop) because of this mistake. Just make sure you've done your homework regarding pricing since you won't be able to change it without altering the cover.

And now we will get to the third thing that is important to these stores, people! Yes, they need readers in the store to generate sales. In 2020, bookshops did everything they could to hang on and offer their books online and for curbside delivery. While the realities of quarantine have kept people out of the shop, bookstore owners know that they make sales when people come in and look around. As restrictions have eased the number of readings, book club meetings, and events hosted by local bookstores have increased. Foot traffic is critical to the success of these shops.

The successful store owners have their own methods of driving foot traffic to the store. When you contact them and make the ask, you'll need to bring some ideas of your own as well as a track record for driving people to the store. There are several things you need to do in order to make this an easy "yes" for the store owner. First, get to know them. Attend the events they regularly put on. Participate in their book club. Connect with the other patrons. Then it makes it easy for them to support you as part of their community. You'll also want to either work with them for a launch party and show evidence of past sales or connect with them after the book has been released and let them know how many sales the book has generated. They want to help you, but remember, they really want to drive in-store sales as well.

After all is said and done, even with the best strategy in place the store may have an entire extra box of your books that just aren't moving. That is precious inventory space that they need to use for books that are going to sell. Which means, those books have to go somewhere. As business owners, the bookshop is going to want to be able to send those books back and get a refund. Which means that your books need to be returnable. It's not ideal for anyone involved, but it is the reality of selling in retail. Shelf space is a limited commodity. Before a bookstore will even order your books, they will first check to see that you are accepting returns. That way they aren't stuck with inventory that they need to give away at a loss in order to make space in their store room.

Your Brick-And-Mortar Retail Strategy

Now that we know what bookstores want, you have to decide if you have the drive and energy to pursue this strategy. Remember, this isn't an all or nothing option. You can decide to not pursue this strategy right now as you transition from Amazon-only to wide and then come back to this opportunity later on.

The first thing you will need to do to ensure this strategy is available to you is what you are already taking care of: getting your books out wide and off the Amazon-only strategy. Amazon is killing brick-and-mortar book sales. Amazon doesn't allow you to set a wholesale discount or set your books as "returnable." Calling up your local bookstore and saying, "well, my book is available on Amazon," is like calling up Burger King and asking for a BigMac. It's kind of a slap in the face.

Instead, you'll want to have your print books available through IngramSpark. Not only can you list a wholesale discount and set your books as returnable, but many brick-and-mortar stores will already have their orders run through the Ingram database. This makes it incredibly easy for the store to order your books if and when the time is right.

One strategy you may need to employ to prove to the store that you can drive sales for them is to work on a consignment basis for a limited time. This is where you provide a few copies of your book to a bookstore and let them put it on the shelf. When a sale is made the store gets a set percent and you get the rest. That means you need to have enough copies of your book on hand and be willing to part with a few knowing that you won't get paid until they sell. Many local bookstores will be familiar with this strategy. Before you agree, you'll want to run the numbers again to make sure you are still getting something for each sale. After all, at this point you will have already paid for the book and shipping to your home as well as any additional costs involved in getting the books to the store owner.

I would try to partner this setup with a book signing or reading event. Otherwise, there won't be much attention on your title.

Does getting your book into stores sound like a lot of work? That's because it is! But, if you are willing to put in the effort, you can realize this dream. Just don't count on this being the most lucrative aspect of your business.

We'll talk more about the marketing process for big-box bookstores in Part 4. For now, just know that if you have any aspirations towards pursuing this strategy, you will need your print books with IngramSpark.

Libraries

This topic is very special to me. And it may be to you as well. I have loved the library since I was a little girl. It was a magical place where I could learn anything. I could find any book I wanted to read. I could retreat into the air conditioning in the summer and travel to other worlds. All for free!

When it was time to release my books into the world, libraries were at the top of my priority list. Because of this lifelong love of libraries, I went wide before that was a thing. Many of the blogs and websites I found back in 2015 were talking about Amazon and the benefits of being exclusive. Without the dedication to seeing my books in libraries, I might have gone the Amazon-only route.

In general, an Amazon-only strategy will not get you into libraries. For your eBooks and Audiobooks, there is no way for the library to purchase a license to distribute your book. If a library has five patrons who want to read your eBook or listen to your Audiobook in a given month, they don't want to pay for the book every time it is checked out. They want to pay one up-front fee to be able to lend it out at will or they want to pay a discount per-use fee. Amazon does not give libraries a means to do this. (And if you have followed #Audiblegate, you know that ACX has tried to operate like a library without compensating authors in this model.) For print books, a library may elect to purchase your paperback from Amazon, but this would be an exception, not a rule.

Libraries are a function of your local municipal government. Which means red tape and bureaucracy. Most library systems have rigid procurement requirements which means that librarians have to get new books based on a limited budget and from a specific list of vendors. Most of the time, Amazon is not on that list.

You need your book to be available through an approved distributor (like OverDrive, Libby, Hoopla, Baker&Taylor, or Bibliotheca) and have the ability to charge licensing fees for digital books.

One specific advantage to working with the aggregators discussed in Chapter 3 is that most of them will get your book into these networks. Findaway Voices also allows authors to specifically set a price for libraries when publishing an Audiobook. They provide a recommendation based off the retail price. I usually look at that recommendation and then cut it by a few dollars. Sure, I could make more, but I want to give libraries a bit of a break on the cost.

What Libraries Want

Now that you are in the right network and have the right payment structure, you need to figure out what libraries even want. They have limited shelf space and simply cannot have a copy of every single book on the premises.

In addition to preferred pricing, libraries want to make sure the books in their catalog appeal to their local patrons. If a library purchases your book and no one checks it out for a year, you shouldn't be surprised when you find it on their neighborhood book sale table. You'll need to remind patrons that your book is available.

And on the opposite side of the spectrum, if you have a steady queue of patrons waiting to check your book out it is going to need to withstand some wear-and-tear. Having your book available as a hardcover is a big benefit to libraries. Digital books such as eBooks and Audiobooks won't ever fade, having these formats available to libraries also helps.

Your Library Strategy

Making your books available to libraries at the right price is only the first step. You'll need to let your readers know they can get the book there too. Many authors in the Kindle Unlimited program lament that when they remove their books their readers who are used to not paying for the books will be mad. First, readers with a Kindle Unlimited subscription ARE paying for the books they read through that service with their monthly subscription. Second, they can actually read the books for free through the library. You'll want to prepare your audience to move to this platform and let them know.

Once a new library purchases your book, give them a thank you and shout-out on social media. You'll be surprised how many people will respond with, "hey that's my local library, I'll check that out!"

The most important library for you to focus on first is your local library. Let the librarians know you are a local author or check their website for details on their local author programs. They may have regular fairs and readings that they are looking to promote. They may have a special section of the library for local authors. Build this relationship and focus on how you can help each other. Libraries need programming for the community they serve. You need more people to read your book. It's an easy pairing of incentives.

When your closest friends and superfans ask how they can help support each new book you release, don't forget to mention libraries. Yes, you want pre-orders. Yes, you want reviews. But the easiest and least expensive thing someone can do is ask their library to get a copy of your book.

Now that you know about all the available options, which platforms stick out to you as the best for your book? How many logins do you want to manage? How many times are you willing to upload your book when it is time to publish? How much effort are you willing to dedicate to a brick-and-mortar strategy? I've created a set of worksheets for you to be able to write out your plan at **AuthorYourAmbition.com/Wide**

PART 3

Going Wide

Create and Execute Your Plan

Now that you know all of this, it is time to roll up your sleeves and get to work. This portion of the book is going to be like one of those "choose-your-own-adventure" books. Do you remember those from when you were a kid? You're reading a mystery and Johnny and Sally get to the top of the dark and scary basement. You can skip to one chapter to see what happens if they go in or another one if you think they should stay out.

Depending on what your vision is for your book you may realize that some of the following information isn't relevant. For example, if you already own your ISBNs, you can skip the section on purchasing and assigning those. You already know how to do that. If you don't have your own ISBNs, then be sure to read that section.

Every author is on a unique path and that means we are all arriving at this point with different experiences and different books. Read the sections that apply to you, re-read them if you need to. Don't stress the items that you aren't planning to incorporate into your wide strategy.

CHAPTER 6

Opting out of Exclusivity

Before we can do anything with these other platforms, we first need to make sure you are able to place your books there. Amazon offers multiple incentives to keep your content exclusive to their platform. They do this so they can market the value of their Kindle Unlimited and Audible Exclusive programs. After all, if a reader can only get a certain book through their subscription, they are incentivizing them to stay in that membership. In order to get us authors on board, Amazon has provided us with different programs that can only be accessed when we agree to only sell our books on their channels. It's a win-win for Amazon.

Don't worry, exclusive is not a "til death do us part" situation. You have the option to remove your book from these contracts. We'll discuss each of these programs in this chapter:

- Kindle Select
- Expanded Distribution
- ACX Exclusivity

The first thing that you need to do before you take any action is figure out if you are exclusive with Amazon and ACX or not. You may be thinking, "M.K., I just read this whole book because my books are only with Amazon KDP right now." But having your book only on Amazon and being exclusive to Amazon are two very different things in this situation.

Both Amazon KDP and ACX have programs where authors can elect to be "exclusive" to their platforms. And they provide handsome incentives to do so. Since you are looking to go wide, I'm not going to go into detail about those benefits because you are either already taking advantage of those programs and you know what they are, or you aren't. If the former, you are still reading this book so that tells me those benefits weren't enough to keep you in an exclusive contract with Amazon. If the latter, well you are about to publish your books wide and therefore won't be able to take advantage of these programs. If you are still unsure, I do recommend going wide to broaden your potential reach and not be at the whims of a single point of sale and Amazon's ability to change payouts without any notice.

Kindle Select

For Amazon KDP, their Kindle Select program is available for eBooks. Authors who agree to join Kindle Select will have their books in the Kindle Unlimited catalog. Why not call the program the same thing for authors and readers? That would be too simple. Many authors refer to both sides of this program interchangeably.

Authors typically opt-in to Kindle Select at the time of publication. If your eBook has been with KDP for some time, you may need to go in and check that you are not in this program. If you are, not to worry, you can opt-out every 90 days. Pay careful attention to the date that your current term in Kindle Select will expire. You can opt-out now, but you will need to wait until the current term has passed to publish the eBook on any other platforms.

Amazon Expanded Distribution

Amazon offered expanded distribution for print books published through KDP Print. This option appears on almost every paperback that you upload to the system. There are certain limitations to joining the program, such as trim size and print interior.

The promise of Expanded Distribution is that your book will be available to all bookstores through Amazon. The reality is that more third-party resellers will list your book on Amazon and potentially bid up on your buy button with their own price. This function doesn't get your book into brick-and-mortar bookstores or on to online bookstores. (As we discussed in Chapter 5 you can't set a wholesale discount.) While the promise and wording on the KDP website around Expanded Distribution makes it seem that you could see your book on the shelves at your local store, the reality is that more third party resellers on Amazon list your book on their website, that's it. You won't see your book at Barnes & Noble through this program.

To be clear, Expanded Distribution is not dependent on making your print book exclusive to Amazon KDP. However, the contract does cause some hiccups when you go to post it on other platforms.

When Expanded Distribution was first announced, I was quick to opt in and test it out. I added my novel, *Enemies of Peace*, to the program. I didn't do much to promote it, I just let it ride to see what would happen. After a few months, I saw that one book had been sold through this program and I noticed a bunch of additional listings for my book from sellers all over the world. One was charging $40 for a used copy of my book that was available new for $9.99. I still haven't been able to riddle that one out.

I opted out of the program on my KDP dashboard and went about my business before ultimately finding IngramSpark as a true wide distribution option for my paperback titles. I went to upload my back list of paperback titles and everything went smoothly, until I went to upload *Enemies of Peace*. I got an error message on IngramSpark stating that

ISBN was already in use. This notice didn't pop up with my other paperbacks that were already out on KDP Print. Then it occurred to me, "Oh right, I did Expanded Distribution." I panicked for a moment, thinking that I must have forgotten to take the book out of the program. I checked my KDP dashboard and sure enough, it was not opted into the program. "What gives?"

Even though I was no longer enrolled in the KDP Expanded Distribution program, my print ISBN was still showing as having expanded distribution through Amazon's network. I had to correct this before I listed my book with IngramSpark. If you have at any point in time listed any of your print books with KDP Expanded Distribution and would like to have them distributed wide through IngramSpark (or another print-on-demand distributor) here are the steps you will need to follow:

1. Ensure your print book is no longer in the Expanded Distribution program with KDP. _HER OWN ISBN_
2. Contact Amazon customer service through Author Central and request that the ISBN be released from expanded distribution. Explain that you are looking to list it for expanded distribution with another network. When I sent in this request, I had a confirmation email back from Amazon the same day confirming that this was done.
3. You will need to complete a title transfer with IngramSpark that gives them permission to list the book with them. You can find the form to complete

on the IngramSpark website. (A link to the form is available in the resources section of this book.)

4. After you submit the form to IngramSpark, it can take up to 30 business days for the transfer to go through so be patient. If the title is not showing up in your dashboard after the 30 business days, then be sure to reach out to IngramSpark customer service to ask for a status update.

While KDP Print Expanded Distribution is not an exclusive contract, it acts that way because the system will keep your print book from being listed elsewhere until the title is released.

I was able to make this change for my book because I owned the ISBN. We'll go into that more in the next chapter, so if you used the Amazon provided ISBN for your paperback, hold tight.

ACX Exclusivity

The other exclusivity contract you will need to check is with ACX. Many authors find themselves in an exclusive contract with ACX for different reasons. If you brought your own finished audio files to ACX or entered into a Pay-For-Production deal with a narrator through ACX, you can remove your Audiobook from the exclusive contract after 90 days by submitting a request to ACX. Prior to 2021, the term for exclusivity was seven years with the ability to make the request to remove your titles at one year. The exclusive term is still seven years, but you can request to remove your titles from exclusivity earlier. This is the result of ongoing negotiations with ACX and ALLi (The Alliance of Independent Authors) and TERM (The Equitable Rights Movement). At the time of this publication, they are still actively working to improve terms for authors on the platform.

Some of you will read this last paragraph and think, "great, I can wait 90 days to get the book out of exclusivity." But remember, that only applies if you just had your Audiobook release through ACX in an exclusive contract today. Go back to your dashboard and check the date that the book was approved and distributed. If it is past 90 days from that date, you can go and make the request now.

Now, the rest of you will be thinking, "wait, what about royalty share deals?" That is where things get tricky. So, you agreed to pay the narrator for their time and effort by agreeing to split royalties with them. They only get compensated for the long hours they spent on your book when a sale is made with ACX distribution partners. Because of this, authors who enter a royalty share deal have to opt into an exclusive contract with ACX at the outset. When you decide that you no longer want to have your book distributed exclusively through ACX, the contract isn't just between you and Amazon. There is a third party involved, your narrator.

You can still write to ACX and request to have your book removed. However, you will need to get your narrator to sign off on this. Most likely, and understandably, they will ask for some kind of payment because when you take the book wide, you will get all the royalties moving forward (as the narrator no longer receives royalties). If your Audiobook is not selling well, this narrator has already invested more than they have received back from the book. If the book is selling well, you are proposing a drop in their monthly regular royalties. This is a delicate situation, and you may think to yourself, "yeah, okay I'll leave this book as exclusive with ACX." If you do decide that you really want the book off of ACX then pack your patience as you will need to communicate with all parties involved. Be prepared for your narrator to flat out say no, any response other than that will be better than those expectations.

In my own personal experience, I have a mix. I have one Audiobook on ACX where I brought files that were provided to me by a narrator outside of the platform. I have five (and counting) Audiobooks that I narrated and produced myself. And I have one final Audiobook that is in a royalty share deal. The books that I self-narrated were never exclusive and were published wide right away. The Audiobook that was narrated by a professional outside of the ecosystem is in an exclusive deal and I can remove it at any time. The royalty share deal is exclusive and as of right now, I don't plan to take it out of that contract. That's right, just because 90% of my books are wide in all formats, doesn't mean I have to make them all wide. In this instance, I just don't want to deal with the hassle and financial consequences of making that move. When I get to a phase in my life with more free time, sure.

You'll notice in these two instances (Kindle Select and ACX) that I have referred to both of these programs as contracts because that is what they are. When you click those boxes, you are completing a contract. If you violate that contract and move your titles wide before the contract period has expired, then Amazon has the right to pull your title from their platforms. And it makes sense. So, if you are looking at your Kindle Select time period and thinking that 90 days is just too long, think twice before taking hasty actions. Take the time to do this the right way, you don't want to be that person who just goes back on their word because they are impatient.

Now that you are no longer exclusive you are free to take your book to other platforms... sort of. There is one more item we need to check on before we can start taking action.

CHAPTER 7

Technical Setup

While you may not have ever had your book enrolled in exclusive contracts with Amazon, you still may have some trouble taking your books to other self-publishing platforms. Many authors who elect to only publish through Amazon usually make the decision to use the KDP-provided ISBN.

I can't blame them. It is way easier, free, and if you didn't initially plan to publish your book anywhere else, it makes sense. Why spend the money to own your ISBN when Amazon is just giving them away?

I have always owned my ISBNs, even back when I first started self-publishing. My primary aim at the time was to make sure my books would be accessible to libraries. As I went down the rabbit hole of trying to find out how to get my books into libraries, I soon discovered that books (digital or print) sold on Amazon wouldn't be able to be purchased through libraries. So, I had to find another distribution option. This research led me into the weird world of ISBNs.

Basically, what I learned was that ISBNs provided "for Free" by Amazon could only be used to publish on Amazon. Because they own the ISBN.

That's right. If you elected to go with the "Free" ISBN from KDP, you can't take that number to another self-publishing platform. (This is why I always put the word "Free" in quotation marks. It doesn't cost you any money, but it reduces the options for your book.)

If you already own your ISBNs and have them registered through the correct ISBN agency for your country, then go ahead and skip this section. But if you made use of the KDP ISBN, then we have a bit more work to do.

We don't have a time machine so we can't go back and undo that decision now. But what we can do is get you your own ISBN.

In this chapter we will also discuss barcodes, Library of Congress registration for U.S. authors, and your copyright page. Then we will go into the fun and exciting world of releasing new editions of your book with your shiny new ISBN.

Get Your Own ISBNs

(*only applicable if you didn't have your own ISBN previously*)

For starters, we need to get you set up with an ISBN that you own. For U.S. based authors that can be done through Bowker. If you live outside of the U.S. (again, I live here so this is where my experience has been), go to your search engine and type in "YOUR COUNTRY + ISBN Registration" to search for the official ISBN agency for your country. Do not buy them off of someone on Fiverr, do not send money via PayPal to someone in an online forum or Facebook group to buy one of their ISBNs off of them. The ISBNs are non-transferable and should only be purchased through the official body recognized by your country.

Depending on your country, you may not have to pay one cent for your ISBNs. If you live in the U.S., that is not the case. One single ISBN is $125, a pack of 10 is $295, and a set of 100 is $575. Keep in mind that you will need one ISBN per format. If you already have a back catalog of three books, each with an eBook, paperback, and Audiobook, then you already need up to nine ISBNs. You will start to realize some cost savings as you purchase more. They don't expire. Take a look at your current catalog and the number of books you plan to release in the next year or so and make a purchasing decision based on that.

Once you have the ISBNs in your account you will need to assign the details. This is the title, subtitle, BISAC Categories, author name, format details, etc. If you already had an Amazon pro-vided ISBN for your title, you will need to re-release it as a second edition in order to make the switch to your own ISBN. Be sure to note that this is a second edition when prompted for those details in Bowker (or the ISBN registration agency site for your country). We will go over the additional instructions for how to issue a second edition in the follow-ing pages. For now, just know that you need to input that information.

I recommend keeping a spreadsheet with the details of your books in-cluding the original pub-lication date, the orig-inal ISBN, the second edition release date, the second edition ISBN, the price, and the Library of Congress Number.

Note about BISAC Codes:

After self-publishing with Amazon, you are likely very familiar with their categories. When you upload your book to Amazon you can select two categories for your book and via Author Central you can add up to 10 distinct categories. This is an ex-cellent way to help readers discover your book. Amazon has many very niche categories to help readers find exactly what they are looking for. Their category model extends be-yond books and helps customers find just about anything on their website. In the larger world of publishing, BISAC (Book Industry Standards and Communication) codes are the closest corollary to these categories. However, these are totally different. That's right your perfectly cultivated niche Amazon categories will not necessarily translate to the BISAC categories you are asked to select when assigning your ISBN or upload-ing your book to other platforms. For starters, there are only 54 distinct BISAC codes, whereas Amazon has a seemingly endless number of catego-ries. On Amazon you may have been able to assign your book to Fiction > Science Fiction > Time Travel, but within the BISAC categories you may only get as narrow as Fiction > Science Fiction.

As a reminder, you can review step-by-step how-to videos on this process on my YouTube Channel: https://www.you-tube.com/c/MKWilliamsAuthor . I will continue to post updated videos on these processes as the platforms upgrade and change their interfaces.

Barcodes for Print Books

Here is where the real "choose-your-own-adventure" kicks in. If after reading about the brick-and-mortar retail strategy in Chapter 5, you still want to pursue this option, you will need to ensure that your list price is printed on the barcode of your paperback and hardcover books. In order to do that you will need to provide your own barcode to the cover designer. If you do not have any intention to ever try to get your books into brick-and-mortar stores then you can skip ahead as you can use the no-price barcodes provided by your print-on-demand distributors.

You'll note that I mentioned this for your paperback and hardcover formats. Digital products, such as eBooks, don't have barcodes because they never pass over a scanner for inventory or point-of-sale.

In the U.S., Bowker also sells barcodes that can be associated with your ISBNs. These are $25 apiece and once you set the price and download the image file for the barcode, the price cannot be changed. So, it is best to make sure you have really thought about the price. If you want to change the price, you'll need to get a new barcode. Both the ISBN and your price will appear on the barcode and the metadata that you assigned to that specific ISBN in Bowker will flow through into the barcode.

There are some no cost barcode emulators that you can also use; however, they may not pull through all the metadata you assigned to the ISBN.

You will want to have this image file ready to provide to your cover design artist so that they can place this and embed it in the image file for your print cover.

The barcode should be in the bottom half of the back cover. You usually find it in the far-right corner; however, you may elect to have it in the middle or left-aligned.

Library of Congress Numbers

In terms of going wide, my own motivation for pursuing this strategy was so that my books could be available in libraries. I love the library and I wanted my books available to fellow bookworms like myself. Plus, libraries offer a significant sales opportunity. In the U.S., your book needs to have a Library of Congress Control Number in order for it to be eligible for local libraries to purchase it. (You also need to be in library databases like OverDrive, Hoopla, or Baker&Taylor. We discussed the aggregator platforms that have access to these databases in Chapter 3.)

If you have only been available through Amazon until now, you likely do not have your book in any libraries. Some local libraries may have purchased a print copy from Amazon; however, libraries have to go through a procurement process which typically does not include Amazon. Even if you purchased a copy of your own book and then donated it to the library, if it didn't have a Library of Congress Control Number (LCCN), it may have ended up on their community book sale table. The LCCN is a critical number to have to get your book into libraries and keep it there. Libraries look for both an ISBN and LCCN in order to track the books in their catalog and order books. Without an LCCN the library won't purchase the book.

Many Amazon-only authors don't take the step to get this number assigned. Aside from the fact that libraries don't typically purchase from Amazon, the application process for the LCCN requires you to provide the ISBN for your title. If you used the Amazon provided ISBN then you wouldn't know your book ISBN until publication. Theoretically an author could apply for their LCCN at that time, however the book is already published and then they would have to revise their eBook and print files to update the copyright page with the LCCN and then re-publish. This isn't impossible, just very tricky and time consuming, especially if libraries don't purchase from Amazon.

Copyright Page

This leads us to the all-important copyright page of your book. When Amazon provides their templates for print books, the copyright page consists of the © mark and a space for the author to enter their name. That's it. Even for an author who is following an Amazon-only strategy that is insufficient, but it is especially not good enough for us wide authors. As you are taking the time to go back through the book before publishing it on new platforms be sure to insert a proper copyright page in the print and digital formats and update the ISBN and LCCN as needed.

Copyright law and the intricacies of what specific disclaimers and details you will need on your copyright page goes well beyond the scope of this book. I recommend that you read Helen Sedwick's *Self-Publisher's Legal Handbook: The Step-by-Step Guide to the Legal Issues of Self-Publishing* for a more in-depth discussion on this and other legal elements. I have some videos on my YouTube channel that lightly touch this topic, but to get a full understanding you can't do better than Sedwick's guide.

Publishing Second Editions

Choose your own adventure time again:

- *If* you used the Amazon-provided ISBNs for your book(s), and
- *If* you have purchased/acquired your new ISBNs that you own

Then keep reading this section. If you used your own ISBNs from the start then feel free to skip this section. If you used the Amazon-provided ISBN, but have not yet acquired your own, then go and do that before returning to this section.

The reason that you will need to publish a second edition of your book is that you cannot publish the same book in the same format under two different ISBNs. When you have the Amazon provided ISBN, that can only be used on Amazon. You can't take the Amazon ISBN to use on other self-publishing platforms. So, you need a new one, one that you own and can use anywhere you please. That part is easy. But with the restriction that you cannot put the same exact book under a different ISBN, then you need to make it a different book. Don't worry, you don't have to rewrite the whole thing. You'll just need to release a second edition of that book.

Let's look at one specific example to help illustrate this point. Four years ago, you self-published your book on Amazon. You used the Amazon provided ISBN for the eBook and the paperback. Now that you are going wide you want to take that eBook and paperback and distribute them through IngramSpark. You've checked that your eBook is no longer in Kindle Select so you have all the clearance you need to publish the book elsewhere. You have your own ISBNs in your account with Bowker and you are ready to assign them so you can get working on your plan to go wide. Great! Let's assign an ISBN to your paperback first. As you fill the information out with Bowker, you will see a field to enter the edition. Since the very first publication of the book was with Amazon, they hold the ISBN for your first edition. You can't assign a new ISBN to the first edition of the paperback again. This is why you need to create a second edition so that you can register the ISBN that you own for that version of the book.

Taking your manuscript and turning it into an updated second edition doesn't have to be excessively difficult. But you actually have to make an update to the book. You can't keep it exactly the same and just say it is a second edition. The book needs to be at least 10% different from the first edition. This is a general rule of thumb that all publishers follow.

What constitutes a 10% difference? This could be a new bonus chapter at the end of the book promoting the next book in the series if that wasn't complete when you first published the book four years ago. It could just be an added chapter to the book that you originally cut. This could be a new foreword or note from the author reflecting on the success of the book. You could update your cover while you are adding these other elements. You could do all of these things. You could do one of these items. But you need to be able to honestly say that this is a new edition of the book.

The first step in the process of creating a new edition is therefore: making those edits. I would suggest saving a new version of your original MS Word Document (or whichever word processer you used). This way you have one clean version of the first edition and another one for the second edition. You can prove the two are materially different if you ever had to. After you make the necessary changes (including an update to the copyright page with the new

ISBN and a note that this is the second edition), you will need to save the file and convert to the necessary formats.

When you complete the ISBN information in Bowker (or the service that issues ISBNs in your country) you will input that this is a second edition for the eBook, paperback, hardcover, etc. The same question will be asked on each platform that you upload the book to, so be sure to note that this is a second edition on all of them. Do not put this in the title field or otherwise amend the title to your book. For example, when I released a second edition of my first novel, *Nailbiters*, the new edition was still called "*Nailbiters.*" Not "*Nailbiters: Updated and Appended.*" Not "*Nailbiters: 2020.*" You need to ensure that the title and subtitle are exactly the same. We'll discuss why in a few paragraphs.

After you have uploaded your new version on all of the wide platforms that you have selected for your plan, you will upload the new version to Amazon KDP. When I did this, I meticulously researched what available information there was on posting a second edition to Amazon KDP. I felt sure that I had the steps down, but I still sent a message to Amazon Customer Service through Author Central in order to confirm that I had the process correct. This helped me to ensure that I was not missing some new policy that was excluded from my research. It also gave me a "paper trail" should something go wrong.

I've included my communication to Amazon here for you to reference and rephrase for your own purposes:

> I have the sequel to my very first novel done and I'll be submitting it to publish in the next few weeks (yay!) As part of my marketing strategy, I want to add the first few pages to the end of the first book to hook readers on that book. Since I'll be adding another chapter, everything I have read says that will mean the update to the first book in the series will need a new ISBN since it will be a second edition of that book.
>
> My question is, should I update the existing manuscript and then provide the new ISBN on the existing book? Or should I upload it as a new book (with the new ISBN) and then ask for the first and second edition to be linked?
>
> Thank you for your help. I just want to make sure I do this correctly the first time so I don't have to panic email later if I mess it all up.

Response from Amazon:

We appreciate your understanding in publishing the sequel for one of your books with us.

Yes, as you state that you would like to add a chapter to the existing book, it needs to be published as newer version of the book under different ISBN.

In this case, we suggest you not to add any edition number to the new book and proceed with publishing, because two different editions could not be linked.

Once the new (updated) version is "LIVE", you can go ahead and unpublish the older (existing) version so that the older version will not be printed. Upon completing these steps, please reach out to us with the ASINs for both versions of the book so that we will be able to have them linked.

We appreciate your understanding and continued support towards Amazon KDP.

This is why I mentioned a few paragraphs ago that you should not change the title of your book to include "new edition" or the like. In order for Amazon to process the update so that all of your reviews and ratings from the book carry through, you need the two editions to be linked. I don't know about you, but I have worked hard for each and every review my books have received. (Friendly reminder: please rate and review this book when you finish it. Thank you!) I would hate to lose my reviews just for uploading a new version.

Following these precise steps is very technical. If you are ever in doubt of whether or not you are following the correct process: ask! I know many people get frustrated when they have to reach out to customer service for any reason. They don't get the answer they want in the time they think it should take or they just didn't like the answer. But as someone who used to work in a customer service role, I always remember to pack my patience. The person on the other end of the conversation wants to help, they just don't know the intricacies of your exact situation out the gate. Be patient, be kind, and make a plan that includes some buffer for response times. Panic emailing Amazon customer service and demanding an immediate answer or action has never worked for anyone.

One Step at a Time

Now that your books are no longer exclusive with Amazon, they are free to be published on any platform, you own the requisite ISBNs, and you know how to update your book, you can finally start getting to work on going wide.

Will this be easy? Not necessarily. Depending on how many books you have in your back catalog this might take some time. But you are operating a publishing company and greatly increasing the exposure for your top selling author: you!

My recommendation is to take one book and one platform at a time. Once you have a clear plan in place you can start to break down the smaller components and check those off of your list. Checklists are going to be your best friend. As you may have already guessed, I've taken the time to build out checklists that you can download and use as you take your books wide. You can get them at **www. AuthorYourAmbition.com/Wide**

I realize the technical aspects may seem daunting. But utilize the checklists and remember the key components to going wide: purchase your owns ISBNs (one for each format), include barcodes with the list price on the back cover (if you want to be in brick-and-mortar stores), apply for a Library of Congress Number, and include a complete copyright page.

Once you finish getting all of your books out wide to the world, will the royalties just start rolling in? Not necessarily. Next, we will start to go over the most important aspect of going wide: marketing.

PART 4

Marketing for Success

The phrase "if you build it, they will come," has been used by many business owners over the years. Yes, you must create the book first, then the readers will come. Getting your books out wide will result in more sales across these platforms. If you build your wide catalog, the readers will come. But how long it takes them to find you and how many show up is entirely up to your marketing efforts.

You had to market and promote your book to get sales on Amazon, and the same applies for these other platforms as well. In this section we'll go over the critical marketing elements that will help you sell wide after you publish your book outside the Amazon ecosystem.

CHAPTER 8

Building Blocks

Before we dip our toes into the vast ocean of paid advertising for books, we first need to get the basics right. These are the building blocks of your brand and if you don't get these right, no amount of advertising dollars will save your sales.

In this chapter we will focus on the organic methods you can and should leverage to tell the world that your books are available on more platforms. First up is the most basic and simple method, just telling people.

Practice Your New Answer

Before we go into the step-by-step actions that you can take on your website, social media, and with paid ads, we need to erase your memory. Like those shiny metal wands from the *Men in Black* movies, we need to scrub your mind of the following phrase, "You can get it on Amazon." This has likely been your go-to answer when friends, family, and fans have asked where they can buy your book. You've probably said it a hundred times on podcast interviews and when promoting your book out to the world.

There is nothing inherently wrong or inaccurate about this statement. Once you go wide your book is still on Amazon, people can buy it from that retailer. But by giving that answer, you are reinforcing that readers should ONLY look for your book on that platform.

We want people to find your book wherever they are already looking. Hence, this is your new answer to this question: "Anywhere great books are sold," or "Anywhere you find great books."

This does two things:

1. It reinforces that you wrote a great book and they should want to read it. It is just as good as any other book on that platform.
2. It is available anywhere they might look for it. The list of potential retailers is too long for you to detail.

I sometimes spice this answer up with a, "Anywhere you find great books, even check your local library! If they don't already have it, you can ask the librarian to order it." Why? Because I want my books in libraries across the country.

But that won't happen unless I put that message out there, to the readers.

While you may not get asked this question often, you must be prepared with your new and inclusive answer. "Anywhere great books are sold." Because if you keep telling everyone to go to Amazon, then you shouldn't be surprised when all of your sales are still from Amazon. The correct answer to the question of where people can find your book reflects your entire ethos on publishing and distribution. It reflects that you are worthy of being sold on multiple platforms.

For example, when you go to promote your book on social media, if you just link to the Amazon book page, then people will only go to Amazon. Can you instead show them a page with all of their available options? Yes, it is one extra click to get them to the checkout, but you are also giving them more options. Your landing page in this case is answering the question with "anywhere great books are sold."

It will take some time to get used to this and there will be moments when you know it is just easier to say, "Amazon." But you won't realize the benefits of publishing wide if you only tell people about one platform.

Tell the World

Now that you have multiple retailers selling your book, you need to announce it to your audience. There are hundreds of thousands of books out there, each retailer cannot possibly give your book attention when it debuts on their website. Instead, you need to do the promotion. Think of each new distribution platform that you engage as an opportunity to do a little P.R. for your book. "Now available on..." "Guess what? This title just got picked up at..." You've got to tell the world about each new opportunity to purchase the book, and chances are you're going to need to keep reminding them as well. Here are a few things that you can do to make your new presence on these vendors known.

Update Your Platform

First and foremost, you will want to update your website. This goes beyond any direct selling or ecommerce pages that you have for your books (as we established in Chapter 4). You will want to add these to your homepage: "Available anywhere great books are sold!" I also like to add the logo for the big stores and link from there. Most people are visual. They can read that there is a link to Barnes & Noble and Apple Books, or you can use their easily recognized logos that people will be able to identify in a fraction of the time.

In addition to including this on your homepage you will want to put these expanded options on your book specific webpages. For my own books, each has their own specific page on my website. I create my own version of the Universal Book Link that we learned about in Chapter 3 with Books2Read. Because I own my website, I can customize these pages to my liking. This is where I can post the book description, any relevant reviews or awards, and the purchase links for every book. Users can easily navigate to any of my books from the main menu on my website. I have also created specific pages for Books-A-Million, Walmart, and OverDrive. While I don't have these linked in the main navigation, I make use of these links when posting to social media.

Speaking of social media, you will want to ensure that your digital profiles on Twitter and Instagram highlight the best place to purchase your books. Space is limited in these profiles so many authors will create a short code link. When a user clicks on this they are taken to a page with a bunch of quick links to top information. You can visit mine on Twitter and Instagram @1mkwilliams as a reference to see how it looks. I use it to highlight my books, YouTube videos, merchandise, and how to purchase directly from me. You'll find the right mix for you and edit this as needed over time.

Keep Reminding Your Readers

Now that you have this content on your website you can easily promote these additional retailers to your readership. You'll want to do this on a regular basis (within reason). What I suggest doing when you first sign up for your wide platforms is to create a schedule of when you will promote the individual retailers. You'll want to promote on each of your social channels as well as Goodreads. As an author, you have the ability to create "blog posts" to your following on Goodreads. Don't forget to leverage this functionality.

I try to schedule reminders to check out my books on specific retailers every other week. You can automate this by scheduling posts in Facebook Content Manager for your Author Facebook page and directly in the Twitter app. There are online services like Hootsuite and Later.com that also allow you to plan and schedule your social media content ahead of time so that you can get back to writing your next book. If I have other priority content to promote (like a new book launch), I'll pause on the retailer specific content. It's a fine balance and each audience will respond differently. I suggest you test and try out different frequencies until you find what works for you.

You should also ask for reviews on these platforms. While we have all been told countless times to get to some magic number of reviews on Amazon to get their algorithm to work for us, we know that these reviews matter on other retailers as well.

It can feel like we are dentists pulling tooth extractions all day trying to get reviews on Amazon, the thought of doing this for other channels can feel equally daunting. But that still doesn't change the fact that you'll need reviews on those channels as well. Customers are used to reviewing comments and use this in their decision-making process. I will throw in review appreciation posts into my social media mix and highlight a five-star review, the platform it was left on, and then a link to purchase. When I get a great review on Google Play, I'll post the review and ask for more ratings on that site.

As you build up for ARC (advance reader copy) team and loyal super fans, you can ask them to post their reviews to more platforms as a way to help the book get noticed. If one of my readers posts a review on Amazon, I am grateful. If they post to Amazon and Goodreads, wow! I am over the moon. If they take the time to post a review to Barnes and Noble, Google Play, or Walmart—I am beside myself with gratitude and joy. But you won't get those reviews unless you ask and ask often.

Educate Your Audience

Now that you are making the most of your wide distribution and letting your readers know about it, you'll likely start to see some improved sales. But, after the initial blitz, people will revert to what is easy, what is familiar.

Ultimately, you need to explain to your readers why it is important to you to make sales separately from Amazon. Perhaps it is the royalty rate on other platforms, maybe it is the opportunity to support you and a local independent bookstore at the same time. Whatever the benefit, you need to spell it out. I have been fortunate enough to cultivate a following that listens when I explain why I am selling my book through a new vendor and how that benefits both me and the reader. I always try to educate my audience when I can in this order:

1. The value to the reader
2. The value to society/the greater good
3. The value to me

As an example, when Bookshop.org partnered with IngramSpark I was thrilled to have another avenue to offer my books to readers. I made sure to let readers know they could get my books from this retailer with this three-point system:

1. Readers can get my print books from Bookshop.org. An excellent new option. (Same value to the reader.)
2. Purchasing from their local bookstore on this website means small independent businesses can continue to operate and compete with the big online retail giant. (Value to society and their community.)
3. I get the same royalty as an author and it makes me feel good to know my favorite local shops will be supported. (Value to me.)

I use this same method when I ask for reviews as well. Although I modify the first point so that I am making a clear ask of the reader:

1. If you enjoyed X book, please take two minutes to leave a review. (Ask of the reader.)

2. These reviews help new readers discover this book so they can enjoy it too. (Value to others.)
3. Thank you for your support. (Value to me expressed as gratitude.)

While it would be great to have dozens of amazing reviews and hundreds of purchases on different retailers each day, most people are too busy with their own lives to take action. You need to remind them often, you need to give them a reason to take action, and you'll have to show big gratitude when they do finally make that purchase or leave a review. It's not about you anymore, it's all about your reader.

CHAPTER 9

More Platforms, More Marketing

As the saying goes, "more money, more..." Wait, we don't have more money yet.

Yes, being a wide author has allowed me to grow my royalties. For two years now the Amazon ecosystem has only accounted for half of my book royalties. That means the other half comes from my wide platforms. But that didn't happen overnight.

Insert your groan right here. Yep, now that your book is available to a wide audience, you have to spread the word far and wide. You will probably pick up a few sales here and there if you add these platforms and do nothing. But my guess is that if you just upload your book and do nothing, you won't get meaningful sales on those new platforms.

And after a couple of months, you'll say that going wide was a huge mistake and waste of effort and then you'll try to go narrow again. I've heard from authors who have done this. They took their books out of Kindle Unlimited, they went wide, and then were surprised when sales didn't magically appear on other platforms. But they had spent weeks, months, years telling their audience to go find their books on Amazon. So of course, that is where people continued to go.

Now that your book is available everywhere, or at the very least in a few additional retailers, you need to communicate the expanded distribution. I go into a lot of detail on the basics of how to sell your book in *Book Marketing for the First-Time Author*. If you already have your books out on Amazon, I'm assuming that you have a base level of knowledge about how to promote your book on that platform.

The elements we discussed in Chapter 8 apply to Amazon-only authors as well. You have to be prepared with an answer when people ask where they can buy your book. You have to remind them to purchase and review as often as they can stand it. But beyond those building blocks, you now have a wide array (pun intended) of new programs at your disposal to help market your books.

Here are some of the critical steps that you need to take to maximize the *new* offerings for your titles.

New Opportunities

Now that your books are out wide on multiple platforms, you will have access to new marketing initiatives. Kindle Select has tempted many authors to stay exclusive to the Amazon ecosystem with their eBooks because of the marketing tools in the program. But many other platforms, both direct retailers and aggregators, offer some nice tools as well.

Coupon Codes and Limited Time Offers

Pricing is one way to signal value and drive demand for your books. If you can offer a limited time discount or promotional code, you give the readers a reason to buy your book right now. If they don't have a reason to purchase now, they might delay and ultimately forget. But if they know the offer only lasts for a few days then you are giving them a reason to take action while helping them save a little bit of money too! Many of the direct retailers make this available to authors. You can either schedule a price reduction or create a coupon code. That code can be valid for a specific date range or number of redemptions.

Your aggregators may offer sales options as well. For example, Smashwords does several sales throughout the year and authors can opt to participate and lower their prices as part of the sale. These sales are usually themed around a specific genre or season. (ex. Romance or Autumn)

Make the most of your new platforms and make sure you get any newsletters or digests they email out to authors. Be strategic with how you utilize the coupons and sales. A perpetual sale price may work for one author's book, but not another's. Test and try different strategies to see how you can move the needle on your sales.

I like to offer a coupon code for my book, *Self-Publishing for the First-Time Author,* to those who subscribe to my newsletter. This offers them immediate value for subscribing and gets my book in front of a very targeted audience.

BookBubs and Chirp Deals

BookBub Deals are quite a buzzy topic for self-published authors. Many independent authors swear by their efficacy and improved long-term sales and reviews. Whereas others who are starting out will look at the cost of one of these deals and hit the "X" on their browser as fast as they can. Regardless of where you stand on them, it is important to know that as a wide-author you have access to these deals if you ever wanted to give it a try.

Part of these BookBub Deals involves significantly discounting your eBook below the regular price for readers to enjoy the savings. Some of the direct self-publishing platforms provide tools for you to do this. With Amazon, you can only do this with Kindle Select, which means exclusivity. While Kindle Select made it much easier for you as an author to change your eBook price and offer it for free for a limited time, you still have this option as a wide-author. All you need to do is enact the lower price on your other retailers. Once that price reduction is showing, go to Amazon Author Central and ask them to match the lower price. Keep in mind you'll want to do this ahead of when your BookBub deal is scheduled so that you comply with the rules of the promotion and readers can get the deal price the day the offer is mailed out.

For Audiobooks you now have the option to offer price discounts by going wide. With ACX you can get free promotional codes to encourage readers to leave reviews and that's about it. You don't have any price control whatsoever over your Audiobook. Not in setting the list price and certainly not when it comes to any discounts. The only way you can reduce your price on Audible and Amazon for your Audiobook is to offer it at a lower list price through Findaway Voices and message Amazon Author Central to ask them to match the lower price. Beyond posting a permanent lower list price for your Audiobook, you can also set limited time deals and promotions on Findaway Voices. This is a critical step to leveraging BookBub's Chirp Audiobook Deals. This functions in the same way as their eBook deals, but you must first verify that your Audiobook is available through Findaway Voices in order to apply for this deal since you have to be able to control the price of your Audiobook.

Both of these options are in addition to the pay-per-click ads that any author (Amazon-only or Wide) can do via the BookBub ads platform.

Brick-and-Mortar Stores

We are going to choose our own adventure again. If after reading Chapter 5 you have decided that you want your book to be available to brick-and-mortar stores, then you need to do some work to make that happen. Unfortunately, just having everything in place doesn't mean a major box store or local bookstore will just stock your book and prominently display it. You'll have to do some legwork to make it happen, and even with all of this in place there is no guarantee that a store will stock your book. It is ultimately up to the shop owner to decide, but you can do several things to give your book the best chance.

If you listed your book with IngramSpark, there are specific ways to market your book. Beyond the wholesale discount, returnability, and the price on the barcode, you need to convince the store that your book deserves to take up a portion of the limited space on the shelves.

The first things you need to do should already be on your go-wide plan:

- Secure your ISBN that you will own
- Set the wholesale discount to 50% to 55%
- Allow for returns

- Select a competitive price for the book and have that printed on your barcode

Next you need to have a solid marketing and publicity plan. Bookstores want to know that you will drive people into the store. Just as we reviewed in Chapter 5, they want to make a sale. You'll want to put together a one-to-two-page document highlighting your marketing plan. These are the details that need to be included:

- Book cover, title, brief description
- Author biography and accolades
- Advance or editorial reviews
- Audience reach
- ISBN, Distributor, Pricing information

The first item is obvious, you need to tell the store the title of the book and what it is about. This is important to help the store determine if they can even consider the book. If the store has seen a spike in children's book sales and you are pitching a children's book, then you may be at the top of the pile of books to consider. If they have seen a sharp decline in children's books sales, then they know to pass on your book.

Your author biography should be to the point and concise. You may need to tailor it to the specific pitch. If you are asking a local bookstore to consider stocking your title then you may want to highlight how long you have lived in the community and any prominent connections you have to local groups who would be willing to patronize the store to support you. If you are applying to a nation-wide chain you will want to focus on your reach as an author and growth metrics for your genre.

You should include any editorial reviews that you have for your book. If you don't have any that is fine too. You can promote any existing sales and review metrics that you have for the book you are pitching or for your backlist titles. Try to highlight sales off of Amazon. Remember, bookstores do not like Amazon and don't want to risk stocking your book only to see someone pick it up in the store, find it on Amazon, click "purchase", then leave the store. If you've priced it consistent across platforms, a customer should have no issue purchasing it locally.

In terms of your audience reach you will want to include your best metrics. Your newsletter size, your social media following itemized by platform, and any other media that you produce or contribute to (magazines, journals, podcasts, and the like). Only highlight what you have and if you have one metric that is visibly weak, you can omit that. For example, I have a decent following on social media, but the majority of my following is on YouTube. I have a very small newsletter subscriber list in comparison. I would highlight my YouTube following and growth metrics and omit my newsletter in this scenario. But that is my personal reach, yours will be different.

And finally, you need to make it easy for the store to find the information needed to make the purchase. Provide your ISBN for the paperback and hardcover. You'll need to make it clear who your distributor is (likely IngramSpark) as well as the retail discount that you are offering. You should make it clear that you are operating on a print-on-demand basis. I would suggest adding a note that you can do an offset run to meet any orders if you are actually willing to foot that cost. (This would require contacting a print house, pricing out the print run, and handling shipping to the store.)

For your local bookstores you may be able to walk in and drop off this flyer with a copy of your book for consideration. Keep in mind that this store may ask to operate on a consignment basis at first before agreeing to do a larger order. For the largest chains, you will need to follow the specific instructions that they provide. Barnes & Noble, Books-A-Million, and Hudson Booksellers all have specific instructions to follow. You should research and cater your pitch to these corporations appropriately. I would also recommend working with the local branches of these stores as you may be able to set up a one-off relationship as a proof of concept to convince the larger corporation to order the book at more locations.

Links to the existing details for these three retailers are in the Resources section at the end of this book. And that is just barely scratching the surface. Anything in this book is already dated the second I'll hit publish. New strategies, techniques, and platforms are emerging every day to help authors sell more books. It will be up to you to research and decide which ones work best for your book.

NEW HORIZONS

The road from here is "wide" open to you. You own your books and can publish them anywhere you would like. You control what happens next. This is where we part and you set off on your own adventure in the world of self-publishing.

Will "going wide" be the magic elixir to boost your book sales? Will you suddenly be earning enough to quit your day job? No and no, at least not overnight. Getting your book out to more retailers, and ultimately more readers, will mean more work for you as an author.

The self-publishing path has never been one of ease. Those of us who don't mind rolling up our sleeves, getting our hands dirty, and using a little elbow grease are happy to put in the effort. And when you do start to see sales on these other platforms, you'll be surprised just how quickly Amazon becomes a minor player in your overall compensation as an author.

But what works today won't work next year. You're now operating as a publisher, not just someone who clicked "publish" on Amazon. There are new strategies to consider and there is always something new to learn. I encourage you to check out the resources section at the end of this book for more ways to continue learning and growing. Whenever I feel as though my book sales are stuck in a rut, I pick up a book, listen to a new podcast, or join a new group of authors and learn as much as I can.

Best of luck on your wide journey!

BEFORE YOU CLOSE THE BOOK...

Thank you for reading **Going Wide: Self-Publishing Your Book Outside The Amazon Ecosystem.** I hope you enjoyed reading it as much as I enjoyed writing it.

It would be a huge favor to me if you would take a moment to leave a rating or review for the book. This helps other readers discover this guide. Please share your honest impression of the book. (I love rave reviews, but even so-so or meh reviews can help the right reader find this book)

Thank you,

M.K. Williams

ACKNOWLEDGMENTS

I first want to give a big thank you to everyone who is a part of the Author Your Ambition Community. Your questions, your drive, your successes, all inspire me to continue to do better and give more to the aspiring authors out there.

Next, I want to thank those who have been supporting my work. The cliché of the penniless writer persists for a reason, royalties are slim for even the best of us. Those who have taken the time and continued to financially support me through my Buy Me A Coffee membership have helped to keep me going. Thank you so much to Jason, Teresa, and Sheila for your support!

RESOURCES

More questions? Schedule some time to connect with me directly or check out my YouTube Channel.

IngramSpark Calculator:

https://myaccount.ingramspark.com/Portal/Tools/
PubCompCalculator

Pitching Big-Box Bookstores:

https://www.barnesandnobleinc.com/publishers-authors/
sell-your-book-at-barnes-noble/

https://www.booksamillion.com/publishers/books.
html?id=8176265964826#submittitle

https://www.hudsonbooksellers.com/book-submissions

Facebook Groups:

IngramSpark Author Community:
https://www.facebook.com/groups/641752356577267

Wide for the Win:
https://www.facebook.com/groups/556186621558858

YouTube Channels:

M.K. Williams:
https://youtube.com/mkwilliamsauthor

Self-Publishing with Dale:
https://www.youtube.com/selfpublishingwithdale

Keith Wheeler Books:
https://www.youtube.com/c/keithwheelerbooks

Podcasts:

The Creative Penn with Joanna Penn:
https://podcasts.apple.com/gb/podcast/
the-creative-penn-podcast-for-writers/id309426367

Alliance of Independent Authors:
https://podcasts.apple.com/us/podcast/askalli-self-
publishing-advice-podcast/id1080135033?mt=2

The Indy Author:
https://www.theindyauthor.com/podcast.html

Copyright and Legal Items:

Helen Sedwick's *Self-Publisher's Legal Handbook: The Step-by-Step Guide to the Legal Issues of Self-Publishing*

"Guide to Writing a Book Copyright Page" *Kindlepreneur.* July 20, 2021: https://kindlepreneur.com/book-copyright-page-examples-ebook/

LINKS AND REFERENCES

Kobo:

Distribution Reach:
https://www.kobo.com/retailpartners#:~:text=Over%20
12%20million%20readers%20use,for%20a%20
completely%20global%20experience.

Apple:

Payments:
https://itunespartner.apple.com/books/articles/apple-
books-payments-2748

Tax Information:
https://itunespartner.apple.com/books/articles/set-up-
tax-information-in-itunes-connect-2704

Barnes&Noble Press:

Payments:
https://help.barnesandnoble.com/app/bnpress/detail/
a_id/4063

Tax Information:
https://help.barnesandnoble.com/app/answers/detail/a_id/
4270/kw/1099

LuLu:

Payment Terms:
https://help.lulu.com/en/support/solutions/articles/
64000255464-creator-revenue-faq#How-are-creator-re
venues-paid?

Tax Information:
https://help.lulu.com/en/support/solutions/articles/
64000255468-tax-and-withholding-faq#Annual-Tax-Forms

ACX Terms of Service:

https://www.acx.com/help/book-posting-agreement/
201481880

https://help.acx.com/s/article/i-used-royalty-share-to-crea
te-my-audiobook-the-book-is-in-stores-but-now-i-d-like-
to-remove-it-is-this-possible

AudibleGate:

https://www.audiblegate.com/

IngramSpark:

Payments:
https://help.ingramspark.com/hc/en-us/articles/
360036942131-Compensation-Payments-Payment-Sch
edule-and-Instructions-for-Updating-Payment-Information

Smashwords:

Audiobooks:
https://www.smashwords.com/about/supportfaq#
audiobooks

Distribution Network:
https://www.smashwords.com/distribution

Payments:
https://www.smashwords.com/about/supportfaq#Royalties

StreetLib:

Payments:
https://help.streetlib.com/hc/en-us/articles/115004206905-
Getting-paid

Author's Republic

Payments:
https://www.authorsrepublic.com/faqs

Taxes:
https://www.authorsrepublic.com/blog/3/tax-forms-which-form-will-i-receive

BISAC:

https://bisg.org/page/BISACFaQ

Thank you so much for reading *Going Wide: Self-Publishing Your Books Outside The Amazon Ecosystem*. I hope that you enjoyed reading it as much as I enjoyed writing it.

If you found this book helpful, please take a moment to leave a review. This helps other authors find this book to help them on their journey.

Don't forget to visit **AuthorYourAmbition.com/Wide** to claim your planners and worksheets to help you go wide.

CPSIA information can be obtained
at www.ICGtesting.com
Printed in the USA
LVHW020303270921
698794LV00004B/37